C000090023

Thomas Carew

Shearsman Classics Vol. XXII

Titles in the *Shearsman Classics* series:

Collected Poems

Thomas Carew

Shearsman Books

Published in the United Kingdom in 2015 by
Shearsman Books Ltd

www.shearsman.com

ISBN 978-1-84861-439-0

Contents

Introduction

Thomas Carew (pronounced "Carey") was one of the finest poets of the "Tribe of Ben", poets and followers of Ben Jonson (1572-1637) who would frequently meet in a tavern in London. An earlier group involving Jonson used to meet at the Mermaid, on Cheapside, a building destroyed in the Great Fire of London (1666); the self-styled *Tribe* met in several taverns, including the Apollo Room in the Devil Tavern at number 2, Fleet Street, near Middle Temple Lane. The venue, which was demolished in 1787, had been a favourite of Jonson's since 1616. Members of the *Sons* included Robert Herrick (1591-1674), Mildmay Fane (Earl of Westmorland, 1602-1666), Sir John Suckling (1609-1641), Edmund Waller (1606-1687) and Thomas Killigrew (1612-1683).

A fine lyric poet, Carew had the slight misfortune—from the historical perspective—of being a most accomplished writer at a time when literary giants stalked the land. There can be no shame in being thought a lesser figure than poets such as Shakespeare, Jonson, Donne or Marvell, for most writers before or since might well have been thus described.

Carew was born in 1594 or 1595, almost certainly at West Wickham, in Kent, where his parents were then living. His father, Matthew, who was knighted in the first years of the 17th century, descended from a prominent Cornish family—one of his ancestors produced an accomplished English version of Tasso's *Gerusalemme Liberata*—while his mother Alice Ryvers, was the daughter of a past Lord Mayor of London.

Thomas was enrolled at Merton College, Oxford, at the age of thirteen, took his degree in 1611, was made a Cambridge B.A. in 1612, and entered the Middle Temple that same year. He was not to prove an apt student of the Law, however, and in 1613 took up a position with Sir Dudley Carleton, Ambassador to Venice, and husband to Sir Matthew's niece. Thomas would appear to have fulfilled his duties satisfactorily as he was re-engaged by Carleton on his embassy to the Netherlands in 1616. For reasons that are now unclear, but appear to be connected to unflattering observations by Carew in writing, concerning Carleton and his wife, the young man fell out with his benefactor later in 1616, and returned to England.

Failing to find alternative preferment at this stage, Carew did nonetheless find himself involved in various Court-related events, such as the investiture of the future Charles I as Prince of Wales on 4 November 1616. His extra-curricular activities were to draw some opprobrium from his father, who complained in a latter to Carleton in October 1617 of his son's behaviour and referred to his suffering at home from "a new disease com in amongest us"—this is likely to have been syphilis. Sir Matthew died the following year, having seen little improvement in his son's behaviour.

It is likely that Carew's love lyrics began to be written in this first London period, and it is evident that the work of John Donne—widely circulated in manuscript at the time—had an impact on his work, with ideas, images and phrases from Donne's work turning up in the younger man's verses, albeit without the older man's elaborate, even baroque, syntax.

After the death of Sir Matthew, the family sold their London residence, and Lady Carew, together with her elder son, retired to an estate at Middle Littleton, Worcestershire.

In 1619, Thomas joined the entourage of Sir Edward Herbert—later Lord Herbert of Cherbury—on his embassy to Paris. Also part of the company was John Crofts, who became a close friend, and whose family would feature prominently amongst the addressees of Carew's verses over the next several years. Indeed, his much-anthologised country-house poem, 'To Saxham', concerns the Crofts' family home. Thomas was to remain in Paris with Herbert for most of the following five years.

Carew's reputation as a poet grew substantially through the 1620s, and his fame was due not solely to the calibre of the work that he produced. His startling erotic poem, 'A Rapture', was almost certainly written during this period. It can shock even now, when palates are more jaded, but even in the wake of the somewhat dissolute late Jacobean years—James I was succeeded by his son Charles I in 1625—the poem attracted censorious commentary, and was denounced in Parliament.

By the close of the decade Carew had become close to Kit Villiers, Earl of Anglesey and brother of the King's favourite, George Villiers, Duke of Buckingham. Carew was to write two elegies on Buckingham following the latter's assassination in 1628.

Following Buckingham's death Charles began to stamp his own character on the Court, shedding old figures from the Jacobean period and setting a new tone, both in terms of personal morality and artistic endeavour. Carew benefitted from this new wave, thanks no doubt to his friendship with James Hay, first Earl of Carlisle, and his wife Lucy, a close friend of Queen Henrietta Maria. Carew abandoned the style that had produced 'A Rapture' and adopted a chivalric tone that was in keeping with the new Queen's predilections. His efforts were evidently successful in so far as he was appointed a gentleman of the privy chamber in 1630, and was also given the post of sewer-in-ordinary to the King. The sewer's duty was to taste and pass dishes of the food to the King, and thus brought Carew into daily contact with the ruling family. He retained the post until his death.

At the same time Carew kept up his relations with literary circles in London, evidenced by the remarkable poems, 'To Ben Johnson: Upon occasion of his Ode of defiance annex'd to his Play of the New Inn' and 'An Elegie upon the death of the Dean of Pauls, Dr. John Donne' (1633). Carew may well have been staking out his territory here, demonstrating that those two great poets were his literary forefathers, but it is also abundantly clear that his work owes them both a debt. The Donne poem is one that declares great admiration for his predecessor's originality, while the one on Jonson appears to admit, with a wry smile, that the old master's reputation and powers were declining, following the failure of the play mentioned in the title.

In the years subsequent to the great 'Elegy on Donne' Carew became more of a commentator on affairs of state, religion and aesthetics. He also composed a highly successful masque,

Coelum Britannicum—not part of the current volume—which was performed at Whitehall on Shrove Tuesday, 18 February 1634. This was Carew's reworking of a 16th-century staged dialogue by Giordano Bruno, and seems to have been aimed principally at pleasing the royal couple, no doubt ably aided by stage designs from Inigo Jones. Sir Henry Herbert, Master of the Revels, referred to *Coelum Britannicum* as "the noblest masque of my time," but Carew was not to write any further masques; rather it was his protégé, Sir William Davenant, who became the pre-eminent writer of court masques in the latter part of the Caroline era.

Carew's literary star at this point was very much in its ascendant, but the creative fires had evidently burned down, and his output in the following years was much reduced. Thomas Carew died in March 1640, and was buried in Saint Dunstan's-in-the-West on 23 March—a fitting resting place, located in Fleet Street, and a church in which Donne had held a benefice while serving as Dean of St. Paul's. Carew's reputation, like that of many of his immediate contemporaries, and even like that of Donne, declined following his death, as literary fashions changed, but— again, as with many other early 17th-century poets—his star rose again in the 20th century, and his lyric talent was once again celebrated. With good reason.

Tony Frazer

Bibliography

Books

Cælum Britanicum. A Masque at White-Hall in the Banquetting-House, on Shrove-Tuesday-Night, the 18 of February, 1633 (London: Printed for Thomas Walkley, 1634).

Poems. By Thomas Carew Esquire (London: Printed by J. Dawson for Thomas Walkley, 1640; enlarged, 1642; third edition, enlarged, London: Printed for Humphrey Moseley, 1651).

Modern Editions

The Poems of Thomas Carew with His Masque Coelum Britannicum, edited by Rhodes Dunlap (Oxford: Clarendon Press, 1949).

Poems 1640, together with Poems from the Wyburd Manuscript (Facsimile edition, Menston: Scolar Press, 1969).

Poems of Thomas Carew, (The Muse's Library edition, edited by Arthur Vincent. (London: George Routledge & Sons; New York, NY: E.P. Dutton & Co., und.).

Anthologies

Peter Davidson (ed.) *Poetry and Revolution. An Anthology of British and Irish Verse 1625-1660* (Oxford & New York, NY: Oxford University Press, 1998)

Alastair Fowler (ed.), *The New Oxford Book of Seventeenth Century Verse* (Oxford & New York, NY: Oxford University Press, 1991)

Helen Gardner (ed.), *The Metaphysical Poets* (Harmondsworth: Penguin Books, 1957)

Hugh Maclean (ed.), *Ben Jonson and the Cavalier Poets* (New York, NY & London: W.W. Norton & Co., 1974)

H.R. Woudhuysen (ed.) *The Penguin Book of Renaissance Verse* (London: Penguin Books, 1992)

Biographical

The best short introduction to the life and work of Thomas Carew is that by Michael P. Parker at the Poetry Foundation's website. The URL is: http://www.poetryfoundation.org/bio/thomas-carew

POEMS.

By
THOMAS CAREVV
Esquire.

One of the Gentlemen of the
Privie-Chamber, and Sewer in
Ordinary to His Majesty.

LONDON,

Printed by *I. D.* for *Thomas Walkley,*
and are to be sold at the signe of the
flying Horse, between Brittains
Burse, and York-House.
1640.

The Spring

Now that the winter's gone, the earth hath lost
Her snow-white robes, and now no more the frost
Candies the grass, or casts an icy cream
Upon the silver Lake or Crystal stream:
But the warm Sun thaws the benumbed Earth,
And makes it tender, gives a sacred birth
To the dead Swallow; wakes in hollow tree
The drowsy Cuckoo and the Humble-bee;
Now do a choir of chirping Minstrels bring
In triumph to the world, the youthful Spring.
The Valleys, hills, and woods in rich array,
Welcome the coming of the long'd for May.
Now all things smile; only my *Love* doth lour:
Nor hath the scalding Noonday Sun the power,
To melt that marble ice, which still doth hold
Her heart congeal'd, and makes her pity cold.
The Ox, which lately did for shelter fly
Into the stall, doth now securely lie
In open fields; and love no more is made
By the fire side; but in the cooler shade
Amyntas now doth with his *Cloris* sleep
Under a Sycamore, and all things keep
Time with the season, only she doth carry
June in her eyes, in her heart *January*.

To *A. L.*
Persuasions to love

Think not, 'cause men flatt'ring say
Y'are fresh as April sweet as May,
Bright as is the morning star,
That you are so, or though you are
Be not therefore proud, and deem
All men unworthy your esteem.
For being so, you lose the pleasure
Of being fair, since that rich treasure
Of rare beauty, and sweet feature
Was bestow'd on you by nature
To be enjoy'd, and 'twere a sin
There to be scarce, where she hath bin
So prodigal of her best graces;
Thus common beauties, and mean faces
Shall have more pastime, and enjoy
The sport you lose by being coy.
Did the thing for which I sue
Only concern my self, not you,
Were men so fram'd as they alone
Reap'd all the pleasure, women none,
Then had you reason to be scant;
But 'twere a madness not to grant
That which affords (if you consent)
To you the giver, more content
Than me, the beggar; Oh then be
Kind to your self if not to me;
Starve not your self, because you may
Thereby make me pine away;
Nor let brittle beauty make
You your wiser thoughts forsake;
For that lovely face will fail,

Beauty's sweet, but beauty's frail;
'Tis sooner past, 'tis sooner done
Than Summer's rain, or Winter's sun:
Most fleeting when it is most dear,
'Tis gone while we but say 'tis here.
These curious locks, so aptly twin'd,
Whose every hair a soul doth bind,
Will change their aburn hue, and grow
White, and cold as winter's snow.
That eye, which now is *Cupid's* nest
Will prove his grave, and all the rest
Will follow; in the cheek, chin, nose
Nor lily shall be found, nor rose.
And what will then become of all
Those, whom now you servants call?
Like swallows when their summer's done,
They'll fly and seek some warmer Sun.
Then wisely choose one to your friend,
Whose love may, when your beauties end,
Remain still firm: be provident
And think before the summer's spent,
Of following winter; like the Ant,
In plenty hoard for time of scant.
Cull out amongst the multitude
Of lovers, that seek to intrude
Into your favour, one that may
Love for an age, not for a day.
One that will quench your youthful fires,
And feed in age your hot desires.
For when the storms of time have mov'd
Waves on that cheek which was belov'd,
When a fair Lady's face is pin'd,
And yellow spread, where once red shin'd;
When beauty youth, and all sweets leave her,
Love may return, but lover never.

And old folks say there are no pains
Like itch of love in agèd veins.
Oh love me then, and now begin it,
Let us not lose this present minute:
For time and age will work that wrack
Which time or age shall ne'er call back.
The snake each year fresh skin resumes,
And eagles change their agèd plumes;
The faded Rose each spring, receives
A fresh red tincture on her leaves:
But if your beauties once decay,
You never know a second *May*.
Oh, then be wise, and whilst your season
Affords you days for sport do reason;
Spend not in vain your life's short hour,
But crop in time your beauty's flower:
Which will away, and doth together
Both bud, and fade, both blow and wither.

Lips and Eyes

In *Celia's* face a question did arise,
Which were more beautiful, her lips or eyes?
We (said the eyes,) send forth those pointed darts
Which pierce the hardest adamantine hearts.
From us (replied the lips,) proceed those blisses
Which lovers reap by kind words and sweet kisses.
Then wept the eyes, and from their springs did pour
Of liquid oriental pearl a shower.
Whereat the lips mov'd with delight and pleasure,
Through a sweet smile unlock'd their pearly treasure
And bade love judge, whether did add more grace:
Weeping or smiling pearls to *Celia's* face.

A divine Mistress

In nature's pieces still I see
Some error that might mended be;
Something my wish could still remove,
Alter or add; but my fair love
Was fram'd by hands far more divine;
For she hath every beauteous line: .
Yet I had been far happier,
Had Nature, that made me, made her;
Then likeness, might (that love creates)
Have made her love what now she hates:
Yet, I confess, I cannot spare
From her just shape the smallest hair;
Nor need I beg from all the store
Of heaven for her one beauty more:
She hath too much divinity for me,
You Gods, teach her some more humanity.

SONG
A Beautiful Mistress

If when the sun at noon displays
                    His brighter rays,
                    Thou but appear,
He then, all pale with shame and fear,
                    Quencheth his light,
Hides his dark brow, flies from thy sight,
                    And grows more dim
Compar'd to thee, than stars to him.
If thou but show thy face again,
When darkness doth at midnight reign,

The darkness flies, and light is hurl'd
Round about the silent world:
So as alike thou driv'st away
Both light and darkness, night and day.

A cruel Mistress

We read of Kings and Gods that kindly took,
A pitcher fill'd with water from the brook;
But I have daily tender'd without thanks
Rivers of tears that overflow their banks.
A slaughter'd bull will appease angry *Jove*,
A horse the Sun, a Lamb the God of love,
But she disdains the spotless sacrifice
Of a pure heart that at her altar lies.
Vesta is not displeas'd, if her chaste urn
Do with repaired fuel ever burn;
But my Saint frowns though to her honour'd name
I consecrate a never-dying flame.
Th' Assyrian king did none i' th' furnace throw
But those that to his image did not bow;
With bended knees I daily worship her,
Yet she consumes her own idolater.
Of such a Goddess no times leave record,
That burnt the temple where she was ador'd.

SONG
Murdering Beauty

I'll gaze no more on her bewitching face,
Since ruin harbours there in every place:
For my enchanted soul alike she drowns
With calms and tempests of her smiles and frowns.
I'll love no more those cruel eyes of hers,
Which pleas'd or anger'd still are murderers:
For if she dart (like lightning) through the air
Her beams of wrath, she kills me with despair.
If she behold me with a pleasing eye,
I surfeit with excess of joy, and die.

My mistress commanding me
to return her letters

So grieves th' adventurous Merchant, when he throws
All the long toil'd for treasure his ship stows
Into the angry main, to save from wrack
Himself and men, as I grieve to give back
These letters, yet so powerful is your sway,
As if you bid me die I must obey.
Go then blest papers, you shall kiss those hands
That gave you freedom, but hold me in bands,
Which with a touch did give you life, but I
Because I may not touch those hands, must die.
Me thinks, as if they knew they should be sent
Home to their native soil from banishment,
I see them smile, like dying Saints, that know
They are to leave the earth, and tow'rd heaven go.

When you return, pray tell your sovereign
And mine, I gave you courteous entertain;
Each line receiv'd a tear, and then a kiss,
First bath'd in that, it 'scaped unscorch'd from this:
I kiss'd it because your hand had been there
But, 'cause it was not now, I shed a tear.
Tell her no length of time, nor change of air,
No cruelty, disdain, absence, despair;
No nor her steadfast constancy, can deter
My vassal heart from ever hon'ring her.
Though these be powerful arguments to prove
I love in vain; yet I must ever love;
Say, if she frown when you that word rehearse,
Service in prose, is oft call'd love in verse:
Then pray her, since I send back on my part
Her papers, she will send me back my heart.
If she refuse, warn her to come before
The God of Love, whom thus I will implore.
Trav'ling thy country's road (*great God*) I spied
By chance this Lady, and walk'd by her side
From place, to place, fearing no violence,
For I was well arm'd, and had made defence
In former fights, 'gainst fiercer foes, than she
Did at our first encounter seem to be.
But, going farther, every step reveal'd
Some hidden weapon, till that time conceal'd;
Seeing those outward arms, I did begin
To fear, some greater strength was lodg'd within,
Looking into her mind, I might survey
An host of beauties that in ambush lay;
And won the day before they fought the field;
For I unable to resist, did yield.
But the insulting tyrant so destroys
My conquer'd mind, my ease, my peace, my joys
Breaks my sweet sleeps, invades my harmless rest,

Robs me of all the treasure of my breast,
Spares not my heart, nor yet a greater wrong;
For having stol'n my heart, she binds my tongue.
But at the last her melting eyes unseal'd,
My lips, enlarg'd, my tongue, then I reveal'd
To her own ears the story of my harms,
Wrought by her virtues and her beauty's charms;
Now hear (*just judge*) an act of savageness,
When I complain, in hope to find redress,
She bends her angry brow, and from her eye,
Shoots thousand darts, I then well hop'd to die,
But in such sovereign balm, love dips his shot,
That though they wound a heart, they kill it not;
She saw the blood gush forth from many a wound,
Yet fled, and left me bleeding on the ground,
Nor sought my cure, nor saw me since: 'tis true,
Absence, and time, (two cunning Leeches) drew
The flesh together, yet sure though the skin
Be clos'd without, the wound festers within.
Thus hath this cruel Lady, us'd a true
Servant, and subject to her self, and you,
Nor know I (great Love,) if my life be sent
To show thy mercy or my punishment;
Since by the only Magic of thy Art
A lover still may live that wants his heart.
If this indictment fright her, so as she
Seem willing to return my heart to me,
But cannot find it, (for perhaps it may;
'Mongst other trifling hearts, be out oth' way.)
If she repent and would make me amends
Bid her but send me hers, and we are friends.

Secrecy protested

Fear not (dear love) that I'll reveal
Those hours of pleasure we two steal;
No eye shall see, nor yet the sun
Descry, what thou and I have done;
No ear shall hear our love, but we
Silent as the night will be.
The god of love himself (whose dart
Did first wound mine, and then thy heart),
Shall never know, that we can tell
What sweets in stolne embraces dwell.
This only means may find it out,
If, when I die, Physicians doubt
What caus'd my death, and there to view
Of all their judgements which was true,
Rip up my heart, Oh then I fear
The world will see thy picture there.

A prayer to the Wind

Go thou gentle whispering wind,
Bear this sigh; and if thou find
Where my cruel fair doth rest,
Cast it in her snowy breast,
So, inflamed by my desire,
It may set her heart a-fire.
Those sweet kisses thou shalt gain,
Will reward thee for thy pain:
Boldly light upon her lip,
There suck odours, and thence skip
To her bosom; lastly fall

Down, and wander over all.
Range about those Ivory hills,
From whose every part distils
Amber dew; there spices grow,
There pure streams of Nectar flow;
There perfume thy self, and bring
All those sweets upon thy wing:
As thou return'st, change by thy power,
Every weed into a flower;
Turn each Thistle to a Vine,
Make the Bramble Eglantine.
For so rich a booty made,
Do but this, and I am paid.
Thou canst with thy powerful blast
Heat apace, and cool as fast:
Thou canst kindle hidden flame,
And again destroy the same;
Then for pity, either stir
Up the fire of love in her,
That alike both flames may shine,
Or else quite extinguish mine.

Mediocrity in love rejected
SONG

G ive me more love, or more disdain;
  The Torrid, or the frozen Zone,
Bring equal ease unto my pain;
  The temperate affords me none:
Either extreme, of love, or hate,
Is sweeter than a calm estate.

Give me a storm; if it be love,
  Like *Danae* in that golden shower
I swim in pleasure; if it prove
  Disdain, that torrent will devour
My Vulture-hopes; and he's possess'd
Of Heaven, that's but from hell releas'd;
  Then crown my joys, or cure my pain;
  Give me more love, or more disdain.

Good counsel to a young Maid
SONG

Gaze not on thy beauty's pride.
  Tender Maid, in the false tide,
That from Lovers' eyes doth slide.

Let thy faithful Crystal show,
How thy colours come, and go,
Beauty takes a foil from woe.

Love, that in those smooth streams lies,
Under Pity's fair disguise,
Will thy melting heart surprise.

Nets, of Passion's finest thread,
Snaring Poems, will be spread,
All to catch thy maiden-head.

Then beware, for those that cure
Love's disease, themselves endure
For reward, a Calenture.

Rather let the Lover pine,
Than his pale cheek, should assign
A perpetual blush to thine.

To my Mistress sitting by
a Rivers side
An Eddy

Mark, how yond eddy steals away,
From the rude stream into the Bay,
There lock'd up safe, she doth divorce
Her waters from the channel's course,
And scorns the Torrent, that did bring
Her headlong from her native spring.
Now doth she with her new love play,
Whilst he runs murmuring away.
Mark how she courts the banks, whilst they
As amorously their arms display,
T'embrace, and clip her silver waves:
See how she strokes their sides, and craves
An entrance there, which they deny;
Whereat she frowns, threat'ning to fly
Home to her stream, and 'gins to swim
Backward, but from the channel's brim,
Smiling, returns into the creek,
With thousand dimples on her cheek.
    Be thou this Eddy, and I'll make
My breast thy shore, where thou shalt take
Secure repose, and never dream
Of the quite forsaken stream:
Let him to the wide Ocean haste,
There lose his colour, name, and taste;
Thou shalt save all, and safe from him,
Within these arms for ever swim.

SONG
Conquest by flight

L adies, fly from Love's smooth tale,
Oaths steep'd in tears do oft prevail;
Grief is infectious, and the air
Inflamed with sighs, will blast the fair:
Then stop your ears, when lovers cry,
Lest your self weep, when no soft eye
Shall with a sorrowing tear repay
That pity which you cast away.
   Young men fly, when beauty darts
Amorous glances at your hearts:
The fix'd mark gives the shooter aim;
And Ladies' looks have power to maim;
Now 'twixt their lips, now in their eyes,
Wrapp'd in a smile, or kiss, Love lies;
Then fly betimes, for only they
Conquer love that run away.

SONG
To my inconstant Mistress

W hen thou, poor excommunicate
From all the joys of love, shalt see
The full reward, and glorious fate,
   Which my strong faith shall purchase me,
   Then curse thine own inconstancy.

A fairer hand than thine, shall cure
   That heart, which thy false oaths did wound;
And to my soul, a soul more pure

Than thine, shall by Love's hand be bound,
And both with equal glory crown'd.

Then shalt thou weep, entreat, complain
To Love, as I did once to thee;
When all thy tears shall be as vain
As mine were then, for thou shalt be
Damn'd for thy false Apostasy.

SONG
Persuasions to enjoy

If the quick spirits in your eye
Now languish and anon must die;
If every sweet, and every grace,
Must fly from that forsaken face:
Then (*Celia*) let us reap our joys,
Ere time such goodly fruit destroys.

Or, if that golden fleece must grow
For ever, free from aged snow;
If those bright suns must know no shade,
Nor your fresh beauties ever fade;
Then fear not (*Celia*) to bestow
What, still being gather'd, still must grow.
Thus, either Time his Sickle brings
In vain, or else in vain his wings.

A deposition from Love

I Was foretold your rebel sex
    Nor love nor pity knew;
And with what scorn, you use to vex
    Poor hearts, that humbly sue;
Yet I believ'd, to crown our pain,
    Could we the fortress win,
The happy lover sure should gain,
    A paradise within:
I thought love's plagues, like Dragons sate
Only to fright us at the gate.

But I did enter, and enjoy,
    What happy lovers prove;
For I could kiss, and sport, and toy,
    And taste those sweets of love;
Which, had they but a lasting state,
    Or if in *Celia's* breast'
The force of love might not abate;
    Jove were too mean a guest.
But now her breach of faith, far more
Afflicts, than did her scorn before.

Hard fate! to have been once possess'd
    As victor, of a heart,
Achiev'd with labour, and unrest,
    And then forc'd to depart.
If the stout Foe will not resign,
    When I besiege a Town,
I lose, but what was never mine;
    But he that is cast down
From enjoy'd beauty, feels a woe,
    Only deposed kings can know.

Ingrateful beauty threatened

Know, *Celia*, (since thou art so proud,)
  'Twas I that gave thee thy renown:
Thou had'st, in the forgotten crowd
    Of common beauties, liv'd unknown,
Had not my verse exhal'd thy name,
And with it, imp'd the wings of fame.

That killing power is none of thine,
  I gave it to thy voice and eyes:
Thy sweets, thy graces, all are mine;
    Thou art my star, shin'st in my skies;
Then dart not from thy borrow'd sphere
Lightning on him, that fix'd thee there.

Tempt me with such affrights no more,
  Lest what I made I uncreate;
Let fools thy mystic forms adore,
    I'll know thee in thy mortal state:
Wise poets that wrapp'd Truth in tales,
Knew her themselves, through all her veils.

Disdain returned

He that loves a rosy cheek,
  Or a coral lip admires,
Or from star-like eyes doth seek,
  Fuel to maintain his fires;
As old *Time* makes these decay,
So his flames must waste away.

But a smooth and steadfast mind,
   Gentle thoughts and calm desires,
Hearts, with equal love combin'd,
   Kindle never dying fires.
Where these are not, I despise
Lovely cheeks, or lips, or eyes.

No tears, *Celia*, now shall win
   My resolv'd heart, to return;
I have search'd thy soul within,
   And find nought but pride and scorn;
I have learn'd thy arts, and now
   Can disdain as much as thou.
Some power, in my revenge convey
That love to her, I cast away.

A Looking-Glass

That flatt'ring Glass, whose smooth face wears
   Your shadow, which a Sun appears,
Was once a river of my tears.

About your cold heart, they did make
A circle, where the briny lake
Congeal'd, into a crystal cake.

Gaze no more on that killing eye,
For fear the native cruelty
Doom you, as it doth all, to die.

For fear lest the fair object move
Your froward heart to fall in love,
Then you yourself my rival prove.

Look rather on my pale cheeks pin'd,
There view your beauties, there you'll find
A fair face, but a cruel mind.

Be not for ever frozen, coy;
One beam of love, will soon destroy,
And melt that ice, to floods of joy.

An Elegy on the La: *Pen*:
sent to my Mistress out of
France

Let him, who from his tyrant Mistress, did
This day receive his cruel doom, forbid
His eyes to weep that loss, and let him here
Open those flood-gates, to bedew this bier;
So shall those drops, which else would be but brine,
Be turn'd to Manna, falling on her shrine.
Let him, who banish'd far from her dear sight
Whom his soul loves, doth in that absence write,
Or lines of passion, or some powerful charms,
To vent his own grief, or unlock her arms;
Take off his pen, and in sad verse bemoan
This general sorrow, and forget his own;
So may those Verses live, which else must die;
For though the Muses give eternity
When they embalm with verse, yet she could give
Life unto that Muse, by which others live.
O, pardon me (fair soul) that boldly have
Dropp'd, though but one tear, on thy silent grave,
And writ on that earth, which such honour had,
To clothe that flesh, wherein thy self was clad.

And pardon me (sweet Saint) whom I adore,
That I this tribute pay, out of the store
Of lines, and tears, that's only due to thee;
Oh, do not think it new Idolatry;
Though you are only sovereign of this Land,
Yet universal losses may command
A subsidy from every private eye,
And press each pen to write; so to supply
And feed the common grief; if this excuse
Prevail not, take these tears to your own use,
As shed for you; for when I saw her die,
I then did think on your mortality;
For since nor virtue, will, nor beauty, could
Preserve from Death's hand this their heavenly mould.
Where they were framed all, and where they dwelt,
I then knew you must die too, and did melt
Into these tears: but thinking on that day,
And when the gods resolv'd to take away
A Saint from us; I that did know what dearth
There was of such good souls upon the earth,
Began to fear lest Death, their Officer,
Might have mistook, and taken thee for her;
So had'st thou robb'd us of that happiness
Which she in heaven, and I in thee possess.
But what can heaven to her glory add?
The praises she hath dead, living she had,
To say she's now an Angel, is no more
Praise than she had, for she was one before;
Which of the Saints can show more votaries
Than she had here? even those that did despise
The Angels, and may her now she is one,
Did whilst she lived with pure devotion
Adore, and worship her; her virtues had
All honour here, for this world was too bad
To hate, or envy her, these cannot rise

So high, as to repine at Deities:
But now she's 'mongst her fellow Saints, they may
Be good enough to envy her, this way
There's loss i' th' change 'twixt heaven and earth, if she
Should leave her servants here below, to be
Hated of her competitors above;
But sure her matchless goodness needs must move
Those blest souls to admire her excellence;
By this means only can her journey hence
To heaven prove gain, if as she was but here
Worshipp'd by men, she be by Angels there.
But I must weep no more over this urn,
My tears to their own channel must return;
And having ended these sad obsequies,
My Muse must back to her old exercise,
To tell the story of my martyrdom:
But, oh thou Idol of my soul, become
Once pitiful, that she may change her style,
Dry up her blubber'd eyes, and learn to smile.
Rest then blest soul, for, as ghosts fly away,
When the shrill Cock proclaims the infant-day,
So must I hence, for lo I see from far,
The minions of the Muses coming are,
Each of them bringing to thy sacred Hearse
In either eye a tear, each hand a Verse.

To my Mistress in absence

Though I must live here, and by force
    Of your command suffer divorce;
Though I am parted, yet my mind,
(That's more my self) still stays behind;
I breathe in you, you keep my heart;

'Twas but a carcase that did part.
Then though our bodies are dis-join'd,
As things that are to place confined;
Yet let our boundless spirits meet,
And in love's sphere each other greet;
There let us work a mystic wreath,
Unknown unto the world beneath;
There let our clasp'd loves sweetly twin;
There let our secret thoughts unseen,
Like nets be weav'd and inter-twin'd,
Wherewith we'll catch each other's mind.
There whilst our souls do sit and kiss,
Tasting a sweet, and subtle bliss
(Such as gross lovers cannot know,
Whose hands, and lips, meet here below;)
Let us look down, and mark what pain
Our absent bodies here sustain,
And smile to see how far away
The one, doth from the other stray;
Yet burn, and languish with desire
To join, and quench their mutual fire.
There let us joy to see from far,
Our emulous flames at loving war,
Whilst both with equal lustre shine,
Mine bright as yours, yours bright as mine.
There seated in those heavenly bowers,
We'll cheat the lag, and ling'ring hours,
Making our bitter absence sweet,
Till souls, and bodies both, may meet.

To her in absence
A SHIP

Toss'd in a troubled sea of griefs, I float
Far from the shore, in a storm-beaten boat;
Where my sad thoughts do (like the compass) show
The several points from which cross-winds do blow.
My heart doth like the needle touch'd with love,
Still fix'd on you, point which way I would move.
You are the bright Pole-star, which in the dark
Of this long absence, guides my wand'ring barque.
Love is the Pilot, but o'er-come with fear
Of your displeasure, dares not homewards steer;
My fearful hope hangs on my trembling sail;
Nothing is wanting but a gentle gale,
Which pleasant breath must blow from your sweet lip,
Bid it but move, and quick as thought this Ship
Into your arms, which are my port, will fly
Where it for ever shall at Anchor lie.

SONG
Eternity of love protested

How ill doth he deserve a lover's name,
Whose pale weak flame,
Cannot retain
His heat, in spite of absence or disdain;
But doth at once, like paper set on fire,
Burn, and expire!
True love can never change his seat,
Nor did he ever love that could retreat.

That noble flame, which my breast keeps alive,
Shall still survive,
When my soul's fled;
Nor shall my love die, when my body's dead,
That shall wait on me to the lower shade,
And never fade:
My very ashes in their urn,
Shall, like a hallowed Lamp, for ever burn.

Upon some alterations in my Mistress, after my departure into *France*

Oh, gentle Love, do not forsake the guide
Of my frail Barque, on which the swelling tide
Of ruthless Pride
Doth beat, and threaten wrack from every side.
Gulfs of disdain, do gape to overwhelm
This boat, nigh sunk with grief,whilst at the helm
Despair commands;
And round about, the shifting sands
Of faithless love and false inconstancy,
With rocks of cruelty,
Stop up my passage to the neighbour Lands.

My sighs have raised those winds, whose fury bears
My sails o'er-board, and in their place spreads tears;
And from my tears
This sea is sprung, where nought but Death appears;
A misty cloud of anger, hides the light
Of my fair star, and every where black night
Usurps the place

Of those bright rays, which once did grace
My forth-bound Ship: but when it could no more
    Behold the vanish'd shore,
In the deep flood she drown'd her beamy face.

Good counsel to a young
Maid

When you the Sun-burnt Pilgrim see
    Fainting with thirst, haste to the springs;
Mark how at first with bended knee
    He courts the crystal Nymph, and flings
    His body to the earth, where He
Prostrate adores the flowing Deity.

But when his heated face is drench'd
    In her cool waves, when from her sweet
Bosom, his burning thirst is quench'd;
    Then mark how with disdainful feet
    He kicks her banks, and from the place
That thus refresh'd him, moves with sullen pace.

So shalt thou be despis'd, fair Maid,
    When by the sated lover tasted;
What first he did with tears invade,
    Shall afterwards with scorn be wasted;
    When all thy Virgin-springs grow dry.
Then no stream shall be left, but in thine eye.

Celia Bleeding, to the Surgeon

Fond man, that canst believe her blood
 Will from those purple channels flow;
Or that the pure untainted flood
  Can any foul distemper know;
Or that thy weak steel can incise
The Crystal case, wherein it lies:

Know; her quick blood, proud of his seat,
  Runs dancing through her azure veins;
Whose harmony no cold, nor heat
  Disturbs, whose hue no tincture stains;
And the hard rock wherein it dwells,
The keenest darts of Love repels.

But thou reply'st, behold, she bleeds;
  Fool! thou'rt deceiv'd; and dost not know
The mystic knot whence this proceeds,
  How Lovers in each other grow;
Thou struckst her arm, but 'twas my heart
Shed all the blood, felt all the smart.

To *T. H.* a Lady resembling
my Mistress

Fair copy of my Celia's face,
 Twin of my soul, thy perfect grace
Claims in my love an equal place.

Disdain not a divided heart,
Though all be hers, you shall have part;
Love is not tied to rules of art.

For as my soul first to her flew,
Yet stay'd with me; so now 'tis true
It dwells with her, though fled to you.

Then entertain this wand'ring guest,
And if it love, allow it rest;
It left not, but mistook the nest.

Nor think my love, or your fair eyes,
Cheaper, 'cause from the sympathies
You hold with her, these flames arise.

To Lead, or Brass, or some such bad
Metal, a Prince's stamp may add
That value, which it never had:

But to the pure refined Ore;
The stamp of Kings imparts no more
Worth, than the metal held before,

Only the Image gives the rate,
To Subjects of a foreign state:
'Tis priz'd as much for its own weight.

So though all other hearts resign
To your pure worth, yet you have mine
Only because you are her coin.

To Saxham

Though frost, and snow, lock'd from mine eyes,
    That beauty which without door lies,
Thy gardens, orchards, walks, that so

I might not all thy pleasures know;
Yet, *Saxham*, thou within thy gate,
Art of thy self so delicate;
So full of native sweets, that bless
Thy roof with inward happiness;
As neither from, nor to thy store
Winter takes aught, or Spring adds more.
The cold and frozen air had sterv'd
Much poor, if not by thee preserv'd,
Whose prayers have made thy Table blest
With plenty, far above the rest.
The season hardly did afford
Coarse cates unto thy neighbours' board,
Yet thou hadst dainties, as the sky
Had only been thy Volary;
Or else the birds, fearing the snow
Might to another deluge grow:
The Pheasant, Partridge, and the Lark
Flew to thy house, as to the Ark.
The willing Ox, of himself came
Home to the slaughter, with the Lamb,
And every beast did thither bring
Himself, to be an offering.
The scaly herd, more pleasure took,
Bath'd in thy dish, than in the brook:
Water, Earth, Air, did all conspire,
To pay their tributes to thy fire,
Whose cherishing flames themselves divide
Through every room, where they deride
The night, and cold abroad; whilst they
Like suns within, keep endless day.
Those cheerful beams send forth their light,
To all that wander in the night,
And seem to beckon from aloof,
The weary Pilgrim to thy roof;

Where if, refresh'd, he will away,
He's fairly welcome, or if stay,
Far more, which he shall hearty find
Both from the Master and the Hind.
The strangers welcome, each man there
Stamp'd on his cheerful brow doth wear;
Nor doth this welcome, or his cheer
Grow less, 'cause he stays longer here.
There's none observes (much less repines)
How often this man sups or dines.
Thou hast no Porter at thy door
T'examine, or keep back the poor;
Nor locks, nor bolt; thy gates have bin
Made only to let strangers in;
Untaught to shut, they do not fear
To stand wide open all the year;
Careless who enters, for they know,
Thou never didst deserve a foe;
And as for thieves, thy bounty's such;
They cannot steal, thou giv'st so much.

Upon a Ribband

This silken wreath, which circles in mine arm,
Is but an Emblem of that mystic charm,
Wherewith the magic of your beauties binds
My captive soul, and round about it winds
Fetters of lasting love; This hath entwin'd
My flesh alone, That hath empal'd my mind:
Time may wear out These soft weak bands; but Those
Strong chains of brass, Fate shall not discompose.
This holy relic may preserve my wrist,
But my whole frame doth by That power subsist:

To That my prayers and sacrifice, to This
I only pay a superstitious kiss:
This but the idol, That's the Deity,
Religion there is due; Here, ceremony.
That I receive by faith, This but in trust;
Here I may tender duty, There I must;
This order as a Layman I may bear,
But I become Love's Priest when That I wear.
This moves like air; that as the Centre stands:
That knot your virtue tied; This but your hands:
That Nature fram'd, but This was made by Art;
This makes my arm your prisoner, That my heart.

To the King, at his entrance into *Saxham*, by Master *Jo. Crofts*

SIR,
Ere you pass this threshold, stay.
And give your creature leave to pay
Those pious rites, which unto you,
As to our household Gods, are due.

In stead of sacrifice, each breast
Is like a flaming Altar, dress'd
With zealous fires, which from pure hearts
Love mixed with loyalty imparts.

Incense, nor gold have we, yet bring
As rich, and sweet an offering;
And such as doth both these express,
Which is our humble thankfulness.
By which is paid the All we owe
To gods above, or men below.

The slaughter'd beast, whose flesh should feed
The hungry flames, we, for pure need
Dress for your supper, and the gore
Which should be dash'd on every door.
We change into the lusty blood
Of youthful Vines, of which a flood
Shall sprightly run through all our veins,
First to your health, then your fair trains.
    We shall want nothing but good fare,
To show your welcome, and our care;
Such rarities, that come from far,
From poor men's houses banish'd are;
Yet we'll express in homely cheer,
How glad we are to see you here.
We'll have what e'er the season yields,
Out of the neighbouring woods, and fields;
For all the dainties of your board
Will only be what those afford;
And, having supp'd, we may perchance
Present you with a country dance.
    Thus much your servants, that bear sway
Here in your absence, bade me say,
And beg besides, you'd hither bring,
Only the mercy of a King;
And not the greatness, since they have
A thousand faults must pardon crave,
But nothing that is fit to wait
Upon the glory of your state.
Yet your gracious favour will,
They hope, as heretofore, shine still
On their endeavours, for they swore
Should *Jove* descend, they could no more.

Upon the sickness of (*E. S.*)

Must she then languish, and we sorrow thus,
And no kind god help her, nor pity us?
Is justice fled from heaven? can that permit
A foul deformed ravisher to sit
Upon her Virgin cheek, and pull from thence
The Rose-buds in their maiden excellence?
To spread cold paleness on her lips, and chase
The frighted Rubies from their native place?
To lick up with his searching flames, a flood
Of dissolv'd Coral, flowing in her blood;
And with the damps of his infectious breath,
Print on her brow moist characters of death?
Must the clear light, 'gainst course of nature cease
In her fair eyes, and yet the flames increase?
Must fevers shake this goodly tree, and all
That ripen'd fruit from the fair branches fall.
Which Princes have desired to taste? must she
Who hath preserv'd her spotless chastity
From all solicitation, now at last
By Agues and diseases be embrac'd?
Forbid it holy *Dian*; else who shall
Pay vows, or let one grain of Incense fall
On thy neglected Altars, if thou bless
No better this thy zealous Votaress?
Haste then, O maiden Goddess, to her aid,
Let on thy quiver her pale cheek be laid;
And rock her fainting body in thine arms;
Then let the God of Music, with still charms,
Her restless eyes in peaceful slumbers close,
And with soft strains sweeten her calm repose.
Cupid descend; and whilst *Apollo* sings,
Fanning the cool air with thy panting wings,

Ever supply her with refreshing wind;
Let thy fair mother, with her tresses bind
Her labouring temples, with whose balmy sweat,
She shall perfume her hairy Coronet,
Whose precious drops, shall upon every fold
Hang, like rich Pearls about a wreath of gold:
Her looser locks, as they unbraided lie,
Shall spread themselves into a Canopy:
Under whose shadow let her rest secure
From chilling cold, or burning Calenture;
Unless she freeze with ice of chaste desires,
Or holy Hymen kindle nuptial fires.
And when at last Death comes to pierce her heart,
Convey into his hand thy golden dart.

A New-Year's Sacrifice
to *Lucinda*

Those that can give, open their hands this day,
   Those that cannot, yet hold them up to pray;
That health may crown the seasons of this year,
And mirth dance round the circle, that no tear
(Unless of joy) may with its briny dew,
Discolour on your cheek the rosy hue;
That no access of years presume to abate,
Your Beauty's ever-flourishing estate:
Such cheap, and vulgar wishes, I could lay
As trivial offerings at your feet this day;
But that it were Apostasy in me,
To send a prayer to any Deity
But your divine self, who have power to give
Those blessings unto others, such as live

Like me, by the sole influence of your eyes,
Whose fair aspects govern our destinies.
   Such Incense, vows, and holy rites, as were
To the involved Serpent of the year
Paid by Egyptian Priests, lay I before
Lucinda's sacred shrine, whilst I adore
Her beauteous eyes, and her pure Altar's dress
With gums and spice of humble Thankfulness;
   So may my Goddess from her heaven, inspire
My frozen bosom with a Delphic fire,
And then the world shall by that glorious flame,
Behold the blaze of thy immortal name.

SONG

To one who, when I praised
my Mistress's beauty, said I
was blind.

Wonder not though I am blind,
            For you must be
Dark in your eyes, or in your mind,
            If, when you see
Her face, you prove not blind like me.
If the powerful beams that fly
            From her eye,
And those amorous sweets that lie
Scatter'd in each neighbouring part,
Find a passage to your heart;
Then you'll confess your mortal sight
Too weak for such a glorious light;
For if her graces you discover,
You grow, like me, a dazzled lover;
But if those beauties you not spy,
Then are you blinder far than I.

SONG

To my Mistress, I burning
in love

I Burn, and cruel you, in vain
Hope to quench me with disdain;
If from your eyes, those sparkles came,
That have kindled all this flame,
What boots it me, though now you shroud
Those fierce Comets in a cloud?
Since all the flames that I have felt,
Could your snow yet never melt,
Nor, can your snow (though you should take
Alps into your bosom) slake
The heat of my enamour'd heart.
But with wonder learn Love's art:
No seas of ice can cool desire,
Equal flames must quench Love's fire:
Then think not that my heat can die,
Till you burn as well as I.

SONG

To her again, she burning
in a fever

Now she burns as well as I,
Yet my heat can never die;
She burns, that never knew desire,
She that was ice, she now is fire.
She whose cold heart, chaste thoughts did arm

So, as Love's flames could never warm
The frozen bosom where it dwelt,
She burns, and all her beauties melt;
She burns, and cries, Love's fires are mild;
Fevers are God's, and He's a child.
Love, let her know the difference
'Twixt the heat of soul and sense.
Touch her with thy flames divine,
So shalt thou quench her fire, and mine.

Upon the King's sickness

Sickness, the minister of death, doth lay
So strong a siege against our brittle clay,
As, whilst it doth our weak forts singly win,
It hopes at length to take all man-kind in.
First, it begins upon the womb to wait,
And doth the unborn child there uncreate;
Then rocks the cradle where the infant lies,
Where, ere it fully be alive, it dies.
It never leaves fond youth, until it have
Found, or an early, or a later grave.
By thousand subtle sleights from heedless man,
It cuts the short allowance of a span.
And where both sober life, and Art combine
To keep it out, Age makes them both resign.
Thus, by degrees, it only gain'd of late,
The weak, the agèd, or intemperate;
But now the Tyrant hath found out a way
By which the sober, strong, and young decay:
Ent'ring his royal limbs that is our head,
Through us his mystic limbs the pain is spread,
That man that doth not feel his part, hath none

In any part of his dominion;
If he hold land, that earth is forfeited,
And he unfit on any ground to tread.
This grief is felt at Court, where it doth move
Through every joint, like the true soul of love.
All those fair stars, that do attend on Him,
Whence they deriv'd their light, wax pale and dim.
That ruddy morning beam of Majesty,
Which should the Sun's eclipsed light supply,
Is overcast with mists, and in the lieu
Of cheerful rays sends us down drops of dew:
That curious form, made of an earth refin'd,
At whose blest birth, the gentle Planets shin'd
With fair aspects, and sent a glorious flame
To animate so beautiful a frame;
That Darling of the Gods and men, doth wear
A cloud on's brow, and in his eye a tear:
And all the rest (save when his dread command
Doth bid them move,) like lifeless statues stand;
So full a grief, so generally worn
Shows a good King is sick, and good men mourn.

SONG

To a Lady, not yet enjoy'd
by her Husband

Come *Celia*, fix thine eyes on mine,
    And through those crystals our souls flitting,
Shall a pure wreath of eye-beams twine.
    Our loving hearts together knitting;
Let Eaglets the bright Sun survey,
Though the blind Mole discern not day.

When clear *Aurora* leaves her mate,
  The light of her grey eyes despising,
Yet all the world doth celebrate
  With sacrifice her fair up-rising:
Let Eaglets the bright Sun survey,
Though the blind Mole discern not day.

A Dragon kept the golden fruit,
  Yet he those dainties never tasted;
As others pin'd in the pursuit.
  So he himself with plenty wasted:
Let Eaglets the bright Sun survey,
Though the blind Mole discern not day.

SONG

The willing Prisoner to his Mistress

L et fools great Cupid's yoke disdain,
    Loving their own wild freedom better;
Whilst proud of my triumphant chain
    I sit, and court my beauteous fetter.

Her murd'ring glances, snaring hairs,
  And her bewitching smiles, so please me,
As he brings ruin, that repairs
  The sweet afflictions that disease me.

Hide not those panting balls of snow,
  With envious veils, from my beholding;
Unlock those lips, their pearly row,
  In a sweet smile of love unfolding.

And let those eyes, whose motion wheels
  The restless Fate of every lover,
Survey the pains, my sick heart feels,
  And wounds themselves have made, discover.

A fly that flew into my Mistress her eye

While this Fly liv'd, she us'd to play
  In the bright sunshine all the day;
Till, coming near my *Celia's* sight,
She found a new, and unknown light
So full of glory, as it made
The noon-day Sun a gloomy shade;
At last this amorous Fly became
My rival, and did court my flame.
She did from hand to bosom skip.
And from her breath, her cheek, and lip,
Suck'd all the incense, and the spice,
So grew a bird of Paradise:
At last into her eye she flew,
There scorch'd in flames, and drown'd in dew,
Like *Phaeton* from the Sun's sphere
She fell, and with her dropp'd a tear:
Of which a pearl was straight compos'd.
Wherein her ashes lie enclos'd.
Thus she received from *Celia's* eye
Funeral flame, tomb, Obsequy.

SONG

Celia singing

Hark, how my *Celia,* with the choice
    Music of her hand and voice
Stills the loud wind; and makes the wild
Incensed Boar, and Panther mild!
Mark how those statues like men move,
Whilst men with wonder statues prove!
This stiff rock bends to worship her,
That idol turns idolater.
    Now, see how all the new-inspir'd
Images, with love are fir'd;
Hark how the tender Marble groans,
And all the late transformed stones,
Court the fair Nymph with many a tear,
Which she (more stony than they were)
Beholds with unrelenting mind;
Whilst they amaz'd to see combin'd
Such matchless beauty, with disdain,
Are all turn'd into stones again.

SONG

Celia singing

You that think Love can convey,
        No other way,
But through the eyes into the heart,
        His fatal dart:
Close up those casements, and but hear
        This Siren sing;
        And on the wing

Of her sweet voice, it shall appear
That Love can enter at the ear:
     Then unveil your eyes, behold
          The curious mould
Where that voice dwells, and, as we know,
          When the Cocks crow,
          We freely may
          Gaze on the day;
So may you, when the Music's done
Awake and see the rising Sun.

SONG

To one that desired to know
my Mistress

Seek not to know my love, for she
     Hath vow'd her constant faith to me;
Her mild aspects are mine, and thou
Shalt only find a stormy brow:
For if her beauty stir desire
In me, her kisses quench the fire.
Or, I can to Love's fountain go,
Or dwell upon her hills of snow.
But when thou burn'st, she shall not spare
One gentle breath to cool the air.
Thou shalt not climb those Alps, nor spy
Where the sweet springs of Venus lie;
Search hidden Nature, and there find
A treasure to enrich thy mind;
Discover Arts not yet reveal'd,
But let my Mistress live conceal'd;
Though men by knowledge wiser grow,
Yet here 'tis wisdom not to know.

SONG

In the person of a Lady to her inconstant servant

When on the Altar of my hand,
  (Bedew'd with many a kiss, and tear;)
Thy now revolted heart, did stand
  An humble martyr, thou did'st swear
  Thus; (and the God of Love did hear,)
By those bright glances of thine eye,
Unless thou pity me, I die.

When first those perjur'd lips of thine,
  Bepal'd with blasting sighs, did seal
Their violated faith on mine,
  From the soft bosom that did heal
  Thee, thou my melting heart did'st steal;
My soul, enflam'd with thy false breath,
Poison'd with kisses, suck'd in death.

Yet I nor hand, nor lip will move,
  Revenge, or mercy, to procure
From the offended God of love;
  My curse is fatal, and my pure
  Love, shall beyond thy scorn endure:
If I implore the Gods, they'll find
Thee too ungrateful, me too kind.

Truce in Love intreated

No more, blind God, for see my heart
   Is made thy Quiver, where remains
No void place for another Dart;
And, alas! that conquest gains
Small praise, that only brings away
A tame and unresisting prey.

Behold a nobler foe, all arm'd,
Defies thy weak Artillery,
That hath thy Bow and Quiver charm'd;
A rebel beauty, conquering Thee!
If thou dar'st equal combat try,
Wound her, for 'tis for her I die.

SONG
To my Rival

Hence, vain intruder, haste away,
   Wash not with thy unhallow'd brine
The footsteps of my Celia's shrine;
Nor on her purer Altars lay
Thy empty words, accents that may
   Some looser Dame to love incline;
   She must have offerings more divine;
Such pearly drops, as youthful *May*
Scatters before the rising day;
   Such smooth soft language, as each line
Might stroke an angry God, or stay
   Jove's thunder, make the hearers pine
With envy; do this, thou shalt be
Servant to her, Rival to me.

Boldness in Love

Mark how the bashful morn, in vain
        Courts the amorous Marigold,
With sighing blasts, and weeping rain;
Yet she refuses to unfold.
But when the Planet of the day
Approacheth with his powerful ray,
Then she spreads, then she receives
His warmer beams into her virgin leaves.
So shalt thou thrive in love, fond Boy;
If thy tears, and sighs discover
Thy grief, thou never shalt enjoy
The just reward of a bold lover:
But when with moving accents, thou
Shalt constant faith, and service vow,
Thy *Celia* shall receive those charms
With open ears, and with unfolded arms.

A Pastoral Dialogue

Celia.   *Cleon.*

As *Celia* rested in the shade
        With *Cleon* by her side,
The swain thus courted the young Maid,
        And thus the Nymph replied.

CL.
Sweet! let thy captive, fetters wear,
        Made of thine arms, and hands;
Till such as thraldom scorn, or fear,
        Envy those happy bands.

CE.
Then thus my willing arms I wind
    About thee, and am so
Thy pris'ner; for my self I bind,
    Until I let thee go.

CL.
Happy that slave whom the fair foe
    Ties in so soft a chain.
CE.   'Far happier I, but that I know
    Thou wilt break loose again.

CL.
    By thy immortal beauties, never!
CE.   Frail as thy love's thine oath.
CL.   Though beauty fade, my love lasts ever.
CE.   Time will destroy them both.

CL.
    I dote not on that snow-white skin.
CE.   What then?   *CL.*   Thy purer mind.
CE.   It loved too soon.   *CL.*   Thou had'st not been
    So fair, if not so kind.'

CE.
    Oh strange vain fancy!   *CL.*   But yet true.
CE.   Prove it!   *CL.*   Then make a braid
Of those loose flames, that circle you,
    My sun's, and yet your shade.

CE.
'Tis done.   *CL.*   Now give it me.   *CE.*   Thus thou
    Shalt thine own error find;
If these were beauties, I am now
    Less fair, because more kind.

CL.

You shall confess you err; that hair,
    Shall it not change the hue,
Or leave the golden mountain bare?
CE.   Ay me! it is too true.

CL.

But this small wreath, shall ever stay
    In its first native prime,
And smiling, when the rest decay,
    The triumphs sing of time.

CE.

Then let me cut from thy fair grove,
    One branch, and let that be
An emblem of eternal love,
    For such is mine to thee.

CL.

Thus are we both redeem'd from time,
    I by thy grace.   *CE.*   And I
Shall live in thy immortal rhyme,
    Until the Muses die.

CL.

By heaven!   *CE.*   Swear not; I if I must weep,
    Jove shall not smile at me;
This kiss, my heart, and thy faith keep.
CL.   This breathes my soul to thee.

Then forth the thicket *Thyrsis* rush'd,
    Where he saw all their play;
The swain stood still, and smil'd, and blush'd,
    The Nymph fled fast away.

Grief engross'd

Wherefore do thy sad numbers flow
                    So full of woe?
Why dost thou melt in such soft strains,
                    Whilst she disdains?
    If she must still deny,
    Weep not, but die:
    And in thy Funeral fire
    Shall all her fame expire.
Thus both shall perish, and as thou on thy Hearse
Shall want her tears, so she shall want thy Verse;
    Repine not then at thy blest state,
    Thou art above thy fate;
    But my fair *Celia* will not give
    Love enough to make me live;
    Nor yet dart from her eye
    Scorn enough to make me die.
Then let me weep alone, till her kind breath,
Or blow my tears away, or speak my death.

A Pastoral Dialogue

Shepherd.   Nymph.   Chorus.

Shep. This mossy bank they press'd. *Ny.* That aged Oak
Did canopy the happy pair
    All night from the damp air.
Cho. Here let us sit, and sing the words they spoke,
Till the day breaking, their embraces broke.

                    Shep.
See love, the blushes of the morn appear,
    And now she hangs her pearly store

(Rob'd from the Eastern shore)
I' th' cowslip's bell, and Roses ear:
Sweet, I must stay no longer here.

Nymph.

Those streaks of doubtful light, usher not day,
But show my sun must set: no Morn
Shall shine till thou return,
The yellow Planets, and the grey
Dawn, shall attend thee on thy way.

Shep.

If thine eyes gild my paths, they may forbear
Their useless shine. *Nymph.* My tears will quite
Extinguish their faint light.
She. Those drops will make their beams more clear,
Love's flames will shine in every tear.

Cho.

They kiss'd, and wept, and from their lips, and eyes,
In a mix'd dew of briny sweet,
Their joys and sorrows meet,
But she cries out. *Nymph.* Shepherd arise,
The Sun betrays us else to spies.

Shep.

The winged hours fly fast, whilst we embrace,
But when we want their help to meet,
They move with leaden feet.
Nym. Then let us pinion *Time*, and chase
The day for ever from this place.'

Shep.

Hark!   *Ny.* Ay me, stay!'   *Shep.* For ever.
      Ny. No, arise,

We must be gone.'   *Shep.* My nest of spice!'
Nymph. My soul.   *Shep.* My Paradise.
Cho. Neither could say farewell, but through their eyes
    Grief, interrupted speech with tears' supplies.

Red, and white Roses

R ead in these Roses, the sad story
    Of my hard fate and your own glory:
In the White you may discover
    The paleness of a fainting lover:
In the Red, the flames still feeding
On my heart with fresh wounds bleeding.
    The White will tell you how I languish,
And the Red express my anguish.
    The White my innocence displaying,
The Red my martyrdom betraying.
    The frowns that on your brow resided,
    Have those Roses thus divided.
Oh let your smiles but clear the weather,
And then they both shall grow together.

To my Cousin (C. R.) marrying
my Lady (A.)

H appy Youth, that shalt possess
    Such a spring-tide of delight,
        As the sated Appetite
Shall, enjoying such excess,
Wish the flood of pleasure less;

When the Hymeneal Rite
Is perform'd, invoke the night,
That it may in shadows dress
Thy too real happiness;
        Else (as *Semele*) the bright
Deity, in her full might,
May thy feeble soul oppress.
        Strong perfumes, and glaring light,
        Oft destroy both smell, and sight.

A Lover upon an Accident necessitating his departure, consults with Reason

Lover

Weep not, nor backward turn your beams,
    Fond eyes, sad sighs, lock in your breath,
Lest on this wind, or in those streams
    My griev'd soul fly, or sail to death.
Fortune destroys me if I stay,
Love kills me if I go away:
Since *Love*, and *Fortune*, both are blind,
Come *Reason*, and resolve my doubtful mind.

Reason

Fly! and blind Fortune be thy guide,
    And 'gainst the blinder God rebel,
Thy love-sick heart shall not reside
    Where scorn and self-will'd error dwell;
Where entrance, unto *Truth* is barr'd;
Where *Love* and *Faith* find no reward;
For, my just hand may sometime move
The wheel of *Fortune*, not the sphere of *Love*.

Parting, *Celia* weeps

Weep not (my Dear) for I shall go
Laden enough with mine own woe;
Add not thy heaviness to mine:
Since Fate our pleasures must dis-join,
Why should our sorrows meet? if I
Must go, and lose thy company,
I wish not theirs; it shall relieve
My grief, to think thou dost not grieve.

Yet grieve, and weep, that I may bear
Every sigh, and every tear
Away with me, so shall thy breast
And eyes, discharg'd, enjoy their rest.
And it will glad my heart to see,
Thou art thus loath to part with me.

A Rapture

I will enjoy thee now my *Celia*, come,
And fly with me to Love's Elysium:
The Giant, Honour, that keeps cowards out,
Is but a Masquer, and the servile rout
Of baser subjects only, bend in vain
To the vast idol, whilst the nobler train
Of valiant Lovers, daily sail between
The huge Colossus' legs, and pass unseen
Unto the blissful shore; be bold and wise,
And we shall enter, the grim Swiss denies
Only to tame fools a passage, that not know
He is but form, and only frights in show

The duller eyes that look from far; draw near,
And thou shalt scorn, what we were wont to fear.
We shall see how the stalking Pageant goes
With borrowed legs, a heavy load to those
That made, and bear him; not as we once thought,
The seed of Gods, but a weak model wrought
By greedy men, that seek to enclose the common,
And within private arms empale free woman.
    Come then, and mounted on the wings of love
We'll cut the flitting air, and soar above
The Monster's head, and in the noblest seats
Of those blest shades, quench, and renew our heats.
There shall the Queen of Love, and Innocence,
Beauty and Nature, banish all offence
From our close Ivy twines, there I'll behold
Thy bared snow, and thy unbraided gold;
There, my enfranchis'd hand, on every side
Shall o'er thy naked polish'd Ivory slide.
No curtain there, though of transparent lawn,
Shall be before thy virgin-treasure drawn;
But the rich Mine, to the enquiring eye
Expos'd, shall ready still for mintage lie,
And we will coin young *Cupids*. There, a bed
Of Roses and fresh Myrtles, shall be spread
Under the cooler shade of cypress groves:
Our pillows of the down of *Venus'* Doves,
Whereon our panting limbs we'll gently lay
In the faint respites of our active play;
That so our slumbers, may in dreams have leisure,
To tell the nimble fancy our past pleasure;
And so our souls, that cannot be embrac'd,
Shall the embraces of our bodies taste.
Meanwhile the bubbling stream shall court the shore,
Th'enamoured chirping Wood-choir shall adore
In varied tunes the Deity of Love;

The gentle blasts of Western winds, shall move
The trembling leaves, & through their close boughs breathe
Still Music, whilst we rest our selves beneath
Their dancing shade; till a soft murmur, sent
From souls entranc'd in amorous languishment,
Rouse us, and shoot into our veins fresh fire,
Till we, in their sweet ecstasy expire.
    Then, as the empty Bee, that lately bore
Into the common treasure, all her store,
Flies 'bout the painted field with nimble wing,
Deflow'ring the fresh virgins of the Spring;
So will I rifle all the sweets, that dwell
In my delicious Paradise, and swell
My bag with honey, drawn forth by the power
Of fervent kisses, from each spicy flower.
I'll seize the Rose-buds in their perfum'd bed,
The Violet knots, like curious Mazes spread
O'er all the Garden, taste the ripen'd Cherry,
The warm, firm Apple, tipp'd with coral berry:
Then will I visit, with a wand'ring kiss,
The vale of Lilies, and the Bower of bliss:
And where the beauteous Region both divide
Into two milky ways, my lips shall slide
Down those smooth Alleys, wearing as I go
A tract for lovers on the printed snow;
Thence climbing o'er the swelling *Apennine*,
Retire into thy grove of Eglantine;
Where I will all those ravish'd sweets distil
Through Love's Alembic, and with Chemic skill
From the mix'd mass, one sovereign Balm derive,
Then bring that great *Elixir* to thy hive.
    Now in more subtle wreaths I will entwine
My sinewy thighs, my legs and arms with thine;
Thou like a sea of milk shalt lie display'd,
Whilst I the smooth, calm Ocean, invade

With such a tempest, as when *Jove* of old
Fell down on *Danae* in a storm of gold:
Yet my tall Pine shall in the *Cyprian* strait
Ride safe at Anchor and unload her freight:
My rudder with thy bold hand, like a tried
And skilful Pilot, thou shalt steer, and guide
My Barque into Love's channel, where it shall
Dance, as the bounding waves do rise or fall:
Then shall thy circling arms embrace and clip
My willing body, and thy balmy lip
Bathe me in juice of kisses, whose perfume
Like a religious incense shall consume,
And send up holy vapours, to those powers
That bless our loves, and crown our sportful hours,
That with such Halcyon calmness, fix our souls
In steadfast peace, as no affright controls.
There, no rude sounds shake us with sudden starts,
No jealous ears, when we unrip our hearts,
Suck our discourse in, no observing spies
This blush, that glance traduce; no envious eyes
Watch our close meetings, nor are we betray'd
To Rivals by the bribed chamber-maid.
No wedlock bonds unwreathe our twisted loves;
We seek no midnight Arbour, no dark groves
To hide our kisses, there, the hated name
Of husband, wife, lust, modest, chaste, or shame,
Are vain and empty words, whose very sound
Was never heard in the Elysian ground.
All things are lawful there, that may delight
Nature or unrestrained Appetite;
Like and enjoy, to will, and act, is one,
We only sin when Love's rites are not done.
    The Roman *Lucrece* there reads the divine
Lectures of Love's great master, *Aretine*,
And knows as well as *Lais*, how to move

Her pliant body in the act of love.
To quench the burning Ravisher, she hurls
Her limbs into a thousand winding curls,
And studies artful postures, such as be
Carv'd on the bark of every neighbouring tree
By learned hands, that so adorn'd the rind
Of those fair Plants, which as they lay entwin'd,
Have fann'd their glowing fires. The Grecian Dame,
That in her endless web, toil'd for a name
As fruitless as her work, doth there display
Her self before the youth of *Ithaca*,
And th'amorous sport of gamesome nights prefer,
Before dull dreams of the lost Traveller.
Daphne hath broke her barque, and that swift foot,
Which th'angry gods had fasten'd with a root
To the fix'd earth, doth now unfetter'd run
To meet th'embraces of the youthful Sun:
She hangs upon him, like his Delphic Lyre,
Her kisses blow the old, and breathe new fire:
Full of her God, she sings inspired Lays,
Sweet Odes of love, such as deserve the Bays,
Which she her self was. Next her, *Laura* lies
In *Petrarch's* learned arms, drying those eyes
That did in such sweet smooth-pac'd numbers flow,
As made the world enamour'd of his woe.
These, and ten thousand Beauties more, that died
Slave to the Tyrant, now enlarg'd, deride
His cancell'd laws, and for their time mis-spent
Pay into Love's Exchequer double rent.
    Come then, my *Celia*, we'll no more forbear
To taste our joys, struck with a Panic fear,
But will depose from his imperious sway
This proud *Usurper* and walk free, as they
With necks unyoked; nor is it just that He
Should fetter your soft sex with Chastity,

Whom Nature made unapt for abstinence;
When yet this false Impostor can dispense
With human Justice, and with sacred right,
And maugre both their laws command me fight
With Rivals, or with emulous Loves, that dare
Equal with thine, their Mistress' eyes, or hair:
If thou complain of wrong, and call my sword
To carve out thy revenge, upon that word
He bids me fight and kill, or else he brands
With marks of infamy my coward hands,
And yet religion bids from blood-shed fly,
And damns me for that Act. Then tell me why
This Goblin Honour, which the world adores,
Should make men Atheists, and not women Whores?

Epitaph on the Lady Mary Villiers

The Lady *Mary Villiers* lies
    Under this stone; with weeping eyes
The Parents that first gave her birth,
And their sad Friends, laid her in earth:
If any of them (Reader) were
Known unto thee, shed a tear,
Or if thyself possess a gem,
As dear to thee, as this to them,
Though a stranger to this place,
Bewail in theirs, thine own hard case;
For thou perhaps at thy return
Mayest find thy Darling in an Urn.

An other

The purest soul, that e'er was sent
Into a clayey tenement,
Inform'd this dust, but the weak mould
Could the great guest no longer hold,
The substance was too pure, the flame
Too glorious that thither came:
Ten thousand *Cupids* brought along
A Grace on each wing, that did throng
For place there, till they all oppress'd
The seat in which they sought to rest;
So the fair Model broke, for want
Of room to lodge th'Inhabitant.

An other

This little Vault, this narrow room,
Of Love, and Beauty is the tomb;
The dawning beam that 'gan to clear
Our clouded sky, lies darken'd here,
For ever set to us, by death
Sent to inflame the world beneath;
'Twas but a bud, yet did contain
More sweetness than shall spring again,
A budding star, that might have grown
Into a Sun, when it had blown.
This hopeful beauty, did create
New life in Love's declining state;
But now his Empire ends, and we
From fire, and wounding darts are free:
His brand, his bow, let no man fear,
The flames, the arrows, all lie here.

Epitaph on the Lady *S.*
Wife to Sir *W. S.*

The harmony of colours, features, grace,
Resulting Airs (the magic of a face)
Of musical sweet tunes, all which combin'd
To crown one Sovereign beauty, lies confin'd
To this dark Vault. She was a Cabinet
Where all the choicest stones of price were set;
Whose native colours, and purest lustre, lent
Her eye, cheek, lip, a dazzling ornament:
Whose rare and hidden virtues, did express
Her inward beauties, and mind's fairer dress;
The constant Diamond, the wise Chrysolite,
The devout Sapphire, Emerald, apt to write
Records of Memory, cheerful Agate, grave
And serious Onyx, Topaz, that doth save
The brain's calm temper, witty Amethyst.
This precious Quarry, or what else the list
On *Aaron's* Ephod planted, had, she wore:
One only Pearl was wanting to her store,
Which in her Saviour's book she found express'd
To purchase that, she sold Death all the rest.

Maria Wentworth, Thomæ
Comitis Cleveland, filia præ-
mortuæ prima virgineam
animam exhaluit:
An. Dom. 1632. Æt. suæ 18.

And here the precious dust is laid;
Whose purely-tempered clay was made
So fine, that it the guest betray'd.

Else, the soul grew so fast within,
It broke the outward shell of sin,
And so was hatch'd a Cherubin.

In height, it soar'd to God above;
In depth, it did to knowledge move,
And spread in breadth to general love.

Before, a pious duty shin'd
To Parents, courtesy behind,
On either side, an equal mind,

Good to the Poor, to kindred dear,
To servants kind, to friendship clear,
To nothing but her self, severe.

So, though a Virgin, yet a Bride
To every Grace, she justified
A chaste Polygamy, and died.

Learn from hence (Reader) what small trust
We owe this world, where virtue must,
Frail as our flesh, crumble to dust.

On the Tomb of the Duke of Buckingham

Beatissimis Manibtis charissimi viri Illust^{ma}
Conjunx sic parentavit.

When in the brazen leaves of Fame,
    The life, the death, of *Buckingham*
Shall be recorded, if Truth's hand
Incise the story of our Land,
Posterity shall see a fair
Structure, by the studious care
Of two Kings rais'd, that did no less
Their wisdom, than their Power express;
By blinded zeal (whose doubtful light
Made murder's scarlet robe seem white,
Whose vain-deluding phantoms charm'd
A clouded sullen soul, and arm'd
A desperate hand, thirsty of blood)
Torn from the fair earth where it stood;
So the majestic fabric fell.
His Actions let our Annals tell:
We write no Chronicle; This Pile
Wears only sorrow's face and style,
Which, even the envy that did wait
Upon his flourishing estate,
Turn'd to soft pity of his death,
Now pays his Hearse; but that cheap breath
Shall not blow here, nor th'unpure brine
Puddle those streams that bathe this shrine.
   These are the pious Obsequies,
Dropp'd from his chaste Wife's pregnant eyes
In frequent showers, and were alone
By her congealing sighs made stone,
On which the Carver did bestow
These forms and characters of woe;

So he the fashion only lent,
Whilst she wept all the Monument.

An other

Siste Hospes sive Indigena sive
Advena vicissitudinis rerum
memor pauca pellege

Reader, when these dumb stones have told
In borrow'd speech, what Guest they hold;
Thou shalt confess, the vain pursuit
Of human Glory yields no fruit,
But an untimely Grave. If Fate
Could constant happiness create,
Her Ministers, Fortune and Worth,
Had here that miracle brought forth;
They fix'd this child of Honour, where
No room was left for Hope, or Fear,
Of more, or less: so high, so great
His growth was, yet so safe his seat.
Safe in the circle of his Friends:
Safe in his Loyal heart, and ends:
Safe in his native valiant spirit:
By favour safe, and safe by merit;
Safe by the stamp of Nature, which
Did strength, with shape and Grace enrich:
Safe in the cheerful Courtesies
Of flowing gestures, speech, and eyes:
Safe in his Bounties, which were more
Proportion'd to his mind than store;
Yet, though for virtue he becomes
Involv'd Himself in borrowed sums,

Safe in his care, he leaves betray'd
No friend engag'd, no debt unpaid.
  But though the stars conspire to shower
Upon one Head th'united power
Of all their Graces, if their dire
Aspects, must other breasts inspire
With vicious thoughts, a Murderer's knife
May cut (as here) their Darling's life.
Who can be happy then, if Nature must
To make one Happy man, make all men just?

Four Songs, by way of *Chorus*

to a play, at an entertainment
of the King and Queen, by my
Lord Chamberlain;

The First of Jealousy. Dialogue.

Question

From whence was first this Fury hurl'd,
This Jealousy into the world?
Came she from Hell?' *Ans.* No there doth reign
Eternal hatred, with disdain,
But she the Daughter is of Love,
Sister of Beauty. *Reply.* Then above
She must derive from the third Sphere
Her heavenly off-spring. *Ans.* Neither there.
From those immortal flames, could she
Draw her cold frozen Pedigree.
    Quest. If nor from heaven nor hell, where then
Had she her birth? *An.* In th' hearts of men,
Beauty, and Fear did her create,
Younger than Love, Elder than Hate,
Sister to both, by Beauty's side
To Love, by Fear to Hate, allied:
Despair her issue is, whose race
Of fruitful mischiefs drowns the space
Of the wide earth in a swol'n flood
Of wrath, revenge, spite, rage, and blood.
    Quest. Ah, how can such a spurious line
Proceed from parents so divine?
    An. As streams, which from their Crystal Spring
Do sweet and clear their waters bring,
Yet mingling with the brackish main,
Nor taste, nor colour they retain.

Qu. Yet Rivers 'twixt their own banks flow
Still fresh; can jealousy do so?
    An. Yes, whilst she keeps the steadfast ground
Of Hope and Fear, her equal bound;
Hope sprung from favour, worth, or chance,
Towards the fair object doth advance;
Whilst Fear, as watchful Sentinel
Doth the invading Foe repel;
And Jealousy, thus mix'd, doth prove
The season, and the salt of love:
But when Fear takes a larger scope,
Stifling the child of Reason, Hope,
Then sitting on th'usurped throne,
She like a Tyrant rules alone,
As the wild Ocean unconfin'd
And raging as the Northern-wind.

2.
On Feminine Honour

In what esteem did the Gods hold
    Fair Innocence, and the chaste bed,
When scandal'd virtue might be bold
    Bare-foot upon sharp Cultures, spread
O'er burning coals to march, yet feel
Nor scorching fire, nor piercing steel?

Why, when the hard edg'd Iron did turn
    Soft as a bed of Roses blown,
When cruel flames forgot to burn
    Their chaste pure limbs, should man alone
'Gainst female Innocence conspire
Harder than steel, fiercer than fire?

Oh, hapless sex! Unequal sway
    Of partial Honour! Who may know
Rebels, from subjects that obey,
    When malice can on vestals throw
Disgrace, and Fame fix high repute
On the close shameless Prostitute?

Vain Honour! thou art but disguise,
    A cheating voice, a juggling art,
No judge of virtue, whose pure eyes
    Court her own Image in the heart,
More pleas'd with her true figure there,
Than her false Echo in the ear.

3.
Separation of Lovers

Stop the chafed Boar, or play
    With the Lion's paw, yet fear
        From the Lover's side to tear
Th'Idol of his soul away.

Though Love enter by the sight
    To the heart, it doth not fly
        From the mind, when from the eye
The fair objects take their flight.

But since want provokes desire,
    When we lose what we before
        Have enjoy'd, as we want more,
So is Love more set on fire.

Love doth with an hungry eye
    Gloat on Beauty, and you may

Safer snatch the Tiger's prey.
Than his vital food deny.

Yet though absence for a space,
    Sharpen the keen Appetite,
    Long continuance, doth quite
All Love's characters efface.

For the sense not fed, denies
    Nourishment unto the mind,
    Which with expectation pin'd,
Love of a consumption dies.

4.
Incommunicability of Love

Quest.   By what power was Love confin'd
        To one object? who can bind,
Or fix a limit to a free-born mind?

An. Nature; for as bodies may
    Move at once but in one way,
So nor can minds to more than one love stray.

Reply. Yet I feel a double smart,
    Love's twinn'd flame, his forked dart.
An. Then hath wild lust, not love possess'd thy heart.

Qu. Whence springs Love?'   *An.* From beauty.
    Qu. Why
    Should th'effect not multiply
As fast i' th' heart, as doth the cause i' th' eye?'

An. When two Beauties equal are,
  Sense preferring neither fair,
Desire stands still, distracted 'twixt the pair.

  So in equal distance lay
  Two fair Lambs in the Wolf's way;
The hungry beast will starve ere choose his prey.

  But where one is chief, the rest
  Cease, and that's alone possess'd
Without a Rival, Monarch of the breast.

Songs in the Play

A Lover in the disguise of
an Amazon, is dearly beloved
of his Mistress

Cease, thou afflicted soul, to mourn,
  Whose love and faith are paid with scorn;
For I am starv'd, that feel the blisses
Of dear embraces, smiles, and kisses
From my soul's Idol, yet complain
Of equal love more than disdain.

Cease, Beauty's exile to lament
The frozen shades of banishment,
For I in that fair bosom dwell
That is my Paradise, and Hell;
Banish'd at home, at once at ease,
In the safe Port, and toss'd on Seas.

Cease in cold jealous fears to pine,
Sad wretch, whom Rivals undermine;

For though I hold lock'd in mine arms
My life's sole joy, a Traitor's charms
Prevail, whilst I may only blame
My self, that mine own Rival am.

Another

A Lady, rescued from death by a Knight, who in the instant leaves her, complains thus

O h, whither is my fair Sun fled,
　　Bearing his light, not heat away?
If thou repose in the moist bed
　Of the Sea-Queen, bring back the day
To our dark clime, and thou shalt lie
Bath'd in the sea flows from mine eye.

Upon what whirlwind didst thou ride
　Hence, yet remain fix'd in my heart?
From me, and to me; fled, and tied?
　Dark riddles of the amorous art;
Love lent thee wings to fly, so he
Unfeather'd, now must rest with me.

Help, help, brave youth, I burn, I bleed,
　The cruel God with Bow and Brand
Pursues the life thy valour freed
　Disarm him with thy conquering hand;
And that thou mayest the wild boy tame,
Give me his dart, keep Thou his flame.

To Ben. Johnson

Upon occasion of his Ode of
defiance annex'd to his Play
of the new Inn

'Tis true (dear *Ben*:) thy just chastising hand
   Hath fix'd upon the sotted Age a brand
To their swol'n pride, and empty scribbling due,
It can nor judge, nor write, and yet 'tis true
Thy comic Muse, from the exalted line
Touch'd by thy *Alchemist*, doth since decline
From that her Zenith, and foretells a red
And blushing evening, when she goes to bed,
Yet such, as shall out-shine the glimmering light
With which all stars shall gild the following night.
Nor think it much (since all thy Eaglets may
Endure the Sunny trial) if we say
This hath the stronger wing, or that doth shine
Trick'd up in fairer plumes, since all are thine;
Who hath his flock of cackling Geese compar'd
With thy tun'd choir of Swans? or else who dar'd
To call thy births deformed? but if thou bind
By City-custom or by *Gavel-kind*,
In equal shares thy love on all thy race,
We may distinguish of their sex, and place;
Though one hand form them, & though one brain strike
Souls into all, they are not all alike.
Why should the follies then of this dull age
Draw from thy Pen such an immodest rage,
When thine own tongue proclaims thy itch of praise?
Such thirst will argue drought. No, let be hurl'd
Upon thy works, by the detracting world,
What malice can suggest: let the Rout say,
The running sands that (ere thou make a play)

Count the slow minutes, might a *Goodwin* frame
To swallow when th'hast done thy ship-wreck'd name.
Let them the dear expense of oil upbraid
Suck'd by thy watchful Lamp, that hath betray'd
To theft the blood of martyr'd Authors, spilt
Into thy ink, whilst thou growest pale with guilt.
Repine not at the Taper's thrifty waste,
That sleeks thy terser Poems, nor is haste
Praise, but excuse; and if thou overcome
A knotty writer, bring thy booty home;
Nor think it theft, if the rich spoils so torn
From conquered Authors, be as Trophies worn.
Let others glut on the extorted praise
Of vulgar breath, trust thou to after days:
Thy labour'd works shall live, when Time devours
Th'abortive off-spring of their hasty hours.
Thou art not of their rank, the quarrel lies
Within thine own Verge, then let this suffice,
The wiser world doth greater Thee confess
Than all men else, than Thy self only less.

An Hymeneal Dialogue
Bride and groom

G *room.* Tell me (my Love) since Hymen tied
   The holy knot, hast thou not felt
   A new infused spirit slide
      Into thy breast, whilst mine did melt?

Bride. First tell me (sweet) whose words were those?
   For though your voice the air did break,
   Yet did my soul the sense compose,
      And through your lips my heart did speak.

Groom. Then I perceive, when from the flame
  Of love my scorch'd soul did retire;
Your frozen heart in her place came,
  And sweetly melted in that fire.

Bride. 'Tis true, for when that mutual change
  Of souls was made, with equal gain,
I straight might feel diffus'd a strange,
  But gentle heat through every vein.

Chorus. Oh blest dis-union, that doth so
  Our bodies from our souls divide,
As two do one, and one four grow,
  Each by contraction multiplied.

Bride. Thy bosom then I'll make my nest,
  Since there my willing soul doth perch.
Groom. And for my heart in thy chaste breast,
  I'll make an everlasting search.

Chorus. Oh blest dis-union, &c.

Obsequies to the Lady
ANNE HAY

I heard the Virgins sigh, I saw the sleek
  And polish'd Courtier, channel his fresh cheek
With real tears; the new-betrothed Maid
Smil'd not that day; the graver Senate laid
Their business by; of all the Courtly throng,
Grief seal'd the heart, and silence bound the tongue.
I, that ne'er more of private sorrow knew

Than from my Pen some froward Mistress drew,
And for the public woe, had my dull sense
So sear'd with ever-adverse influence,
As the invader's sword might have unfelt,
Pierc'd my dead bosom, yet began to melt:
Grief's strong instinct, did to my blood suggest
In the unknown loss peculiar interest.
But when I heard the noble *Carlisle's* Gem,
The fairest branch of *Denny's* ancient stem
Was from that Casket stol'n, from this Trunk torn,
I found just cause, why they, why I should mourn.
   But who shall guide my artless Pen, to draw
Those blooming beauties, which I never saw?
How shall posterity believe my story,
If I, her crowded graces, and the glory
Due to her riper virtues, shall relate
Without the knowledge of her mortal state?
Shall I, as once *Apelles*, here a feature,
There steal a Grace, and rifling so whole Nature
Of all the sweets a learned eye can see,
Figure one *Venus*, and say, such was she?
Shall I her legend fill, with what of old
Hath of the Worthies of her sex been told,
And what all pens, and times to all dispense,
Restrain to her, by a prophetic sense?
Or shall I, to the Moral, and Divine
Exactest laws, shape by an even line,
A life so straight, as it should shame the square
Left in the rules of *Katherine* or *Clare*,
And call it hers, say, so did she begin,
And, had she liv'd, such had her progress been?
These are dull ways, by which base pens, for hire,
Daub glorious vice, and from *Apollo's* choir
Steal holy Ditties, which profanely they
Upon the hearse of every strumpet lay.

We will not bathe thy corpse with a forc'd tear,
Nor shall thy train borrow the blacks they wear:
Such vulgar spice, and gums, embalm not thee,
Thou art the theme of Truth, not Poetry.
Thou shalt endure a trial by thy Peers,
Virgins of equal birth, of equal years,
Whose virtues held with thine an emulous strife,
Shall draw thy picture, and record thy life.
One shall ensphere thine eyes, another shall
Impearl thy teeth; a third, thy white and small
Hand shall besnow; a fourth, incarnadine
Thy rosy cheek, until each beauteous line,
Drawn by her hand, in whom that part excels,
Meets in one Centre, where all beauty dwells.
Others, in task shall thy choice virtues share,
Some shall their birth, some their ripe growth declare;
Though niggard *Time* left much unhatch'd by deeds,
They shall relate how thou hadst all the seeds
Of every Virtue, which in the pursuit
Of time, must have brought forth admired fruit.
Thus shalt thou, from the mouth of envy, raise
A glorious journal of thy thrifty days,
Like a bright star, shot from his sphere, whose race
In a continued line of flames, we trace.
This, if survey'd, shall to the view impart
How little more than late, thou wert, thou art,
This shall gain credit with succeeding times,
When nor by bribed pens, nor partial rhymes
Of engag'd kindred, but the sacred truth
Is storied by the partners of thy youth;
Their breath shall Saint thee, and be this thy pride,
Thus even by Rivals to be Deified.

To the Countess of *Anglesey*
upon the immoderately-by-her-
lamented death of her
Husband

Madam, men say, you keep with dropping eyes
Your sorrows fresh, wat'ring the Rose that lies
Fall'n from your cheeks, upon your dear Lord's Hearse.
Alas! those odours now no more can pierce
His cold pale nostril, nor the crimson dye
Present a graceful blush to his dark eye.
Think you that flood of pearly moisture hath
The virtue fabled of old *Æson's* bath?
You may your beauties and your youth consume
Over his Urn, and with your sighs perfume
The solitary Vault, which as you groan,
In hollow Echoes shall repeat your moan;
There you may wither, and an Autumn bring
Upon your self, but not call back his spring.
Forbear your fruitless grief then, and let those
Whose love was doubted, gain belief with shows
To their suspected faith; you, whose whole life
In every act crown'd you a constant Wife,
May spare the practice of that vulgar trade,
Which superstitious custom only made;
Rather, a Widow now, of wisdom prove
The pattern, as a Wife, you were of love:
Yet since you surfeit on your grief, 'tis fit
I tell the world, upon what cates you sit
Glutting your sorrows; and at once include
His story, your excuse, my gratitude.
You, that behold how yond' sad Lady blends
Those ashes with her tears, lest, as she spends
Her tributary sighs, the frequent gust

Might scatter up and down the noble dust,
Know when that heap of Atoms, was with blood
Kneaded to solid flesh, and firmly stood
On stately Pillars, the rare form might move
The froward *Juno's* or chaste *Cynthia's* love.
In motion, active grace, in rest, a calm
Attractive sweetness, brought both wound and balm
To every heart. He was compos'd of all
The wishes of ripe Virgins, when they call
For Hymen's rites, and in their fancies wed
A shape of studied beauties to their bed.
Within this curious Palace dwelt a soul
Gave lustre to each part, and to the whole:
This dress'd his face in courteous smiles; and so
From comely gestures, sweeter manners flow.
This, courage join'd to strength, so the hand, bent,
Was valour's, open'd, Bounty's instrument
Which did the scale, and sword, of Justice hold,
Knew how to brandish steel, and scatter gold.
This taught him, not to engage his modest tongue
In suits of private gain, though public wrong;
Nor mis-employ (*As is the Great Man's use,*)
His credit with his Master, to traduce,
Deprave, malign, and ruin Innocence
In proud revenge of some mis-judg'd offence.
But all his actions had the noble end
T'advance desert, or grace some worthy friend.
He chose not in the active stream to swim,
Nor hunted Honour; which, yet hunted him;
But like a quiet Eddy, that hath found
Some hollow creek, there turns his waters round,
And in continual circles, dances free
From the impetuous Torrent; so did he
Give others leave to turn the wheel of State,
(*Whose restless motion spins the subject's fate*)

Whilst he retir'd from the tumultuous noise
Of Court, and suitors' press; apart, enjoys
Freedom, and mirth, himself, his time, and friends,
And with sweet relish tastes each hour he spends.
I could remember how his noble heart
First kindled at your beauties, with what Art
He chas'd his game through all opposing fears,
When I his sighs to you, and back your tears
Convey'd to him, how loyal then, and how
Constant he prov'd since, to his marriage vow,
So as his wand'ring eyes never drew in
One lustful thought to tempt his soul to sin,
But that I fear such mention rather may
Kindle new grief, than blow the old away.
   Then let him rest, join'd to great *Buckingham*,
And with his brothers, mingle his bright flame:
Look up, and meet their beams, and you from thence
May chance derive a cheerful influence.
Seek him no more in dust, but call again
Your scatter'd beauties home, and so the pen
Which now I take from this sad Elegy,
Shall sing the Trophies of your conquering eye.

An Elegy upon the death of the Dean of Pauls, Dr. John Donne

Can we not force from widowed Poetry,
  Now thou art dead (Great DONNE) one Elegy,
To crown thy Hearse? Why yet dare we not trust,
Though with unkneaded dough-bak'd prose thy dust,
Such as the unscissor'd Churchman from the flower
Of fading Rhetoric, short liv'd as his hour,

Dry as the sand that measures it, should lay
Upon thy Ashes, on the funeral day?
Have we nor voice, no tune? Did'st thou dispense
Through all our language, both the words and sense?
'Tis a sad truth; The Pulpit may her plain,
And sober Christian precepts still retain,
Doctrines it may, and wholesome Uses frame,
Grave Homilies, and Lectures, But the flame
Of thy brave Soul (that shot such heat and light,
As burn'd our earth, and made our darkness bright,
Committed holy Rapes upon our Will,
Did through the eye the melting heart distil;
And the deep knowledge of dark truths so teach,
As sense might judge, what fancy could not reach;)
Must be desir'd for ever. So the fire,
That fills with spirit and heat the Delphic choir,
Which kindled first by thy Promethean breath,
Glow'd here awhile, lies quench'd now in thy death;
The Muses' garden, with Pedantic weeds
O'rspread, was purg'd by thee; The lazy seeds
Of servile imitation thrown away;
And fresh invention planted, Thou did'st pay
The debts of our penurious bankrupt age;
Licentious thefts, that make poetic rage
A Mimic fury, when our souls must be
Possess'd, or with Anacreon's Ecstasy,
Or Pindar's, not their own; The subtle cheat
Of sly Exchanges, and the juggling feat
Of two-edg'd words, or whatsoever wrong
By ours was done the Greek, or Latin tongue,
Thou hast redeem'd, and open'd Us a Mine
Of rich and pregnant fancy, drawn a line
Of masculine expression, which had good
Old Orpheus seen, Or all the ancient Brood
Our superstitious fools admire, and hold

Their lead more precious, than thy burnish'd gold,
Thou hadst been their Exchequer, and no more
They each in other's dust, had rak'd for Ore.
Thou shalt yield no precedence, but of time,
And the blind fate of language, whose tun'd chime
More charms the outward sense; yet thou mayst claim
From so great disadvantage greater fame,
Since to the awe of thy imperious wit
Our stubborn language bends, made only fit
With her tough-thick-ribb'd hoops to gird about
Thy Giant fancy, which had prov'd too stout
For their soft melting Phrases. As in time
They had the start, so did they cull the prime
Buds of invention many a hundred year,
And left the rifled fields, besides the fear
To touch their Harvest, yet from those bare lands,
Of what is only thine, thy only hands
(And that their smallest work) have gleaned more
Than all those times, and tongues could reap before;
    But thou art gone, and thy strict laws will be
Too hard for Libertines in Poetry.
They will repeal the goodly exil'd train
Of gods and goddesses, which in thy just reign
Was banish'd nobler Poems, now, with these
The silenc'd tales o'th'Metamorphoses
Shall stuff their lines, and swell the windy Page,
Till Verse, refin'd by thee, in this last Age
Turn ballad rhyme, Or those old Idols be
Ador'd again, with new apostasy.
    Oh, pardon me, that break with untun'd verse
The reverend silence that attends thy hearse:
Whose awful solemn murmurs were to thee,
More than these faint lines, A loud Elegy,
That did proclaim in a dumb eloquence
The death of all the Arts, whose influence,

Grown feeble, in these panting numbers lies
Gasping short winded accents, and so dies:
So doth the swiftly turning wheel not stand
In th'instant we withdraw the moving hand,
But some small time retain a faint weak course
By virtue of the first impulsive force:
And so whilst I cast on thy funeral pile
Thy crown of Bays, Oh, let it crack a while,
And spit disdain, till the devouring flashes
Suck all the moisture up, then turn to ashes.
 I will not draw thee envy, to engross
All thy perfections, or weep all our loss;
Those are too numerous for an Elegy,
And this too great, to be express'd by me.
Though every pen should share a distinct part,
Yet art thou Theme enough to tire all Art;
Let others carve the rest, it shall suffice
I on thy Tomb this Epitaph incise.

   Here lies a King, that rul'd as he thought fit
   The universal Monarchy of wit;
   Here lie two Flames, and both those, the best,
   Apollo's first, at last, the true God's Priest.

In answer of an Elegiacal Letter
upon the death of the King of
Sweden from *Aurelian Townsend*,
inviting me to write on that subject

Why dost thou sound, my dear *Aurelian*,
 In so shrill accents, from thy *Barbican*,
A loud alarum to my drowsy eyes,

Bidding them wake in tears and Elegies
For mighty *Sweden's* fall? Alas! how may
My Lyric feet, that of the smooth soft way
Of Love, and Beauty, only know the tread,
In dancing paces celebrate the dead
Victorious King, or his Majestic Hearse
Profane with th'humble touch of their low verse?
Virgil, nor *Lucan*, no, nor *Tasso* more
Than both, not *Donne*, worth all that went before,
With the united labour of their wit,
Could a just Poem to this subject fit.
His actions were too mighty to be rais'd
Higher by Verse, let him in prose be prais'd,
In modest faithful story, which his deeds
Shall turn to Poems: when the next Age reads
Of *Frankfurt, Leipzig, Würzburg*, of the *Rhine*,
The *Leck*, the *Danube, Tilly, Wallenstein*,
Bavaria, Papenheim, or *Lutzenfeld*, where he
Gain'd after death a posthume Victory,
They'll think his Acts things rather feign'd than done,
Like our Romances of the Knight o'th' Sun.
Leave we him, then, to the grave Chronicler,
Who, though to Annals he can not refer
His too-brief story, yet his Journals may
Stand by the *Cæsar's* years, and, every day
Cut into minutes, each, shall more contain
Of great designment than an Emperor's reign;
And (since 'twas but his Church-yard) let him have
For his own ashes now no narrower Grave
Than the whole *German* continent's vast womb,
Whilst all her Cities do but make his Tomb.
Let us to supreme providence commit
The fate of Monarchs, which first thought it fit
To rend the Empire from the *Austrian* grasp;
And next from *Sweden's*, even when he did clasp

Within his dying arms the Sovereignty
Of all those Provinces, that men might see
The Divine wisdom would not leave that Land
Subject to any one King's sole command.
Then let the Germans fear, if *Cæsar* shall,
Or the United Princes, rise, and fall,
But let us that in myrtle bowers sit
Under secure shades, use the benefit
Of peace and plenty, which the blessed hand
Of our good King gives this obdurate land,
Let us of Revels sing, and let thy breath
(Which, fill'd Fame's trumpet, with *Gustavus'* death,
Blowing his name to heaven), gently inspire
Thy past'ral pipe, till all our swains admire
Thy song and subject, whilst thou dost comprise
The beauties of the *SHEPHERD'S PARADISE*;
For who like thee (whose loose discourse is far
More neat and polish'd than our Poems are,
Whose very gait's more graceful than our dance)
In sweetly-flowing numbers may advance
That glorious night? When, not to act foul rapes,
Like birds, or beasts, but in their Angel-shapes
A troop of Deities came down to guide
Our steerless barques in passion's swelling tide
By virtue's Card, and brought us from above
A pattern of their own celestial love.
Nor lay it in dark sullen precepts drown'd
But with rich fancy, and clear Action crown'd.
Through a mysterious Fable (that was drawn
Like a transparent veil of purest Lawn
Before their dazzling beauties) the divine
Venus, did with her heavenly *Cupid* shine.
The story's curious web, the Masculine style,
The subtle sense, did Time and sleep beguile,
Pinion'd and charm'd they stood to gaze upon

Th'Angelic forms, gestures, and motion,
To hear those ravishing sounds that did dispense
Knowledge and pleasure, to the soul, and sense.
It fill'd us with amazement to behold
Love made all spirit, his corporeal mould
Dissected into Atoms melt away
To empty air, and from the gross allay
Of mixtures, and compounding Accidents
Refin'd to immaterial Elements.
But when the Queen of Beauty did inspire
The air with perfumes, and our hearts with fire,
Breathing from her celestial Organ sweet
Harmonious notes, our souls fell at her feet,
And did with humble reverend duty, more
Her rare perfections than high state adore.
    These harmless pastimes let my *Townsend* sing
To rural tunes; not that thy Muse wants wing
To soar a loftier pitch, for she hath made
A noble flight, and plac'd th'Heroic shade
Above the reach of our faint flagging rhyme;
But these are subjects proper to our clime.
Tourneys, Masques, Theatres, better become
Our *Halcyon* days; what though the German Drum
Bellow for freedom and revenge, the noise
Concerns not us, nor should divert our joys;
Nor ought the thunder of their Carabins
Drown the sweet Airs of our tun'd Violins;
Believe me friend, if their prevailing powers
Gain them a calm security like ours,
They'll hang their Arms upon the Olive bough,
And dance, and revel then, as we do now.

Upon Master W. Montague
his return from travel

Lead the black Bull to slaughter, with the Boar
And Lamb, then purple with their mingled gore
The Ocean's curled brow, that so we may
The Sea-Gods for their careful waftage pay:
Send grateful Incense up in pious smoke
To those mild spirits, that cast a curbing yoke
Upon the stubborn winds, that calmly blew
To the wish'd shore our long'd for *Mountague*.
Then whilst the Aromatic odours burn,
In honour of their Darling's safe return;
The Muses' Choir shall thus with voice and hand,
Bless the fair Gale that drove his ship to land.

> *Sweetly breathing Vernal Air,*
> *That with kind warmth doest repair*
> *Winter's ruins, from whose breast*
> *All the gums, and spice of th'East*
> *Borrow their perfumes, whose eye*
> *Gilds the morn, and clears the sky,*
> *Whose dishevell'd tresses shed*
> *Pearls upon the Violet bed;*
> *On whose brow, with calm smiles dress'd*
> *The Halcyon sits and builds her nest:*
> *Beauty, Youth, and endless Spring*
> *Dwell upon thy rosy wing.*
> *Thou, if stormy* Boreas *throws*
> *Down whole Forests when he blows,*
> *With a pregnant flowery birth*
> *Canst refresh the teeming Earth;*
> *If he nip the early bud,*
> *If he blast what's fair and good;*

If he scatter our choice flowers,
If he shake our hills or bowers,
If his rude breath threaten us,
Thou canst stroke great Æolus,
And from him the grace obtain
To bind him in an iron chain.

Thus, whilst you deal your body 'mongst your friends,
And fill their circling arms, my glad soul sends,
This her embrace: Thus we of *Delphos* greet,
As Lay-men clasp their hands, we join our feet.

To Master *W. Montague*

Sir, I arrest you at your Country's suit,
Who as a debt to her, requires the fruit
Of that rich stock; which she by Nature's hand
Gave you in trust, to th' use of this whole Land.
Next, she indicts you of a Felony,
For stealing, what was her Propriety:
Your self from hence, so seeking to convey
The public treasure of the state away.
More, you're accus'd of Ostracism, the Fate
Impo'd of old by the Athenian state
On eminent virtue, but that curse which they
Cast on their men, You on your Country lay:
For, thus divided from your noble parts
This Kingdom lives in exile, and all hearts
That relish worth, or honour, being rent
From your perfections, suffer banishment.
These are your public injuries; but I
Have a just private quarrel to defy
And call you Coward, thus to run away

When you had pierc'd my heart, not daring stay
Till I redeem'd my honour; but I swear
By *Celia's* eyes, by the same force to tear
Your heart from you, or not to end this strife
Till I or find revenge, or lose my life.
But as in single fights it oft hath been
In that unequal equal trial seen,
That he who had receiv'd the wrong at first
Came from the Combat oft too with the worst;
So, if you foil me when we meet, I'll then
Give you fair leave to wound me so again.

On the Marriage of *T. K.* and *C. C.* the morning stormy

Such should this day be, so the Sun should hide
His bashful face, and let the conquering Bride
Without a Rival shine, whilst He forbears
To mingle his unequal beams with hers;
Or if sometimes he glance his squinting eye
Between the parting clouds, 'tis but to spy,
Not emulate her glories, so comes dress'd
In veils, but as a Masquer to the feast.
Thus heaven should lour, such stormy gusts should blow
Not to denounce ungentle Fates, but show
The cheerful Bridegroom to the clouds and wind
Hath all his tears, and all his sighs assign'd.
Let Tempests struggle in the Air, but rest
Eternal calms within thy peaceful breast,
Thrice happy Youth; but ever sacrifice
To that fair hand that dried thy blubber'd eyes,

That crown'd thy head with Roses, and turn'd all
The plagues of love into a cordial,
When first it join'd her Virgin snow to thine,
Which, when today the Priest shall recombine,
From the mysterious holy touch such charms
Will flow, as shall unlock her wreathed arms,
And open a free passage to that fruit
Which thou hast toil'd for with a long pursuit.
But ere thou feed, that thou may'st better taste
Thy present joys, think on thy torments past.
Think on the mercy freed thee, think upon
Her virtues, graces, beauties, one by one,
So shaft thou relish all, enjoy the whole
Delights of her fair body, and pure soul.
Then boldly to the fight of Love proceed,
'Tis mercy not to pity though she bleed.
We'll strew no nuts, but change that ancient form,
For till tomorrow we'll prorogue this storm,
Which shall confound, with its loud whistling noise
Her pleasing shrieks, and fan thy panting joys.

For a Picture, where a Queen Laments over the Tomb of a slain Knight

Brave Youth, to whom Fate in one hour
Gave death, and Conquest, by whose power
Those chains about my heart are wound,
With which the Foe my Kingdom bound:
Freed and captiv'd by thee, I bring
For either act an offering;
For victory, this wreath of Bay:

In sign of thraldom, down I lay
Sceptre and crown: take from my sight
Those Royal Robes, since fortune's spite
Forbids me live thy Virtue's prize,
I'll die thy Valour's sacrifice.

To a Lady, that desired I
would love her

1.

Now you have freely given me leave to love,
      What will you do?
   Shall I your mirth or passion move
     When I begin to woo;
Will you torment, or scorn, or love me too?

2.

Each petty Beauty can disdain, and I
      'Spite of your hate
   Without your leave can see, and die;
     Dispense a nobler Fate,
'Tis easy to destroy: you may create.

3.

Then give me leave to love, and love me too:
      Not with design
   To raise, as Love's curs'd Rebels do,
     When puling Poets whine,
Fame to their beauty, from their blubber'd eyne.

4.

Grief is a puddle, and reflects not clear
        Your beauty's rays,
    Joys are pure streams, your eyes appear
        Sullen in sadder lays,
In cheerful numbers they shine bright with praise;

5.

Which shall not mention to express you fair
        Wounds, flames, and darts,
    Storms in your brow, nets in your hair,
        Suborning all your parts,
Or to betray, or torture captive hearts.

6.

I'll make your eyes like morning Suns appear,
        As mild and fair;
    Your brow as Crystal smooth, and clear,
        And your dishevell'd hair
Shall flow like a calm Region of the Air.

7.

Rich Nature's store (which is the Poet's Treasure)
        I'll spend to dress
    Your beauties, if your mine of Pleasure
        In equal thankfulness
You but unlock, so we each other bless.

Upon my Lord Chief Justice
his election of my Lady
A. W. for his Mistress

1.

Hear this, and tremble all
Usurping Beauties, that create
A government Tyrannical,
    In Love's free state,
Justice, hath to the sword of your edg'd eyes
His equal balance join'd, his sage head lies
In Love's soft lap, which must be just and wise.

2.

    Hark! how the stern Law breathes
Forth amorous sighs, and now prepares
No fetters, but of silken wreaths,
    And braided hairs;
His dreadful Rods and Axes are exil'd,
Whilst he sits crown'd with Roses: Love hath fil'd
His native roughness, Justice is grown mild.

3.

    The Golden Age returns!
Love's bow, and quiver, useless lie,
His shaft, his brand, nor wounds, nor burns
    And cruelty
Is sunk to Hell, the fair shall all be kind,
Who loves, shall be belov'd, the froward mind
To a deformed shape shall be confin'd.

4.

Astræa hath possess'd
An earthly seat, and now remains
In *Finch's* heart, but *Wentworth's* breast
That guest contains;
With her she dwells, yet hath not left the skies,
Nor lost her Sphere, for, new-enthron'd, she cries
I know no Heaven but fair *Wentworth's* eyes.

To *A. D.* unreasonable distrust-
ful of her own beauty

Fair *Doris* break thy Glass, it hath perplex'd
   With a dark Comment, beauty's clearest Text;
It hath not told thy face's story true,
But brought false Copies to thy jealous view.
No colour, feature, lovely air, or grace,
That ever yet adorn'd a beauteous face,
But thou mayst read in thine, or justly doubt
Thy Glass hath been suborn'd to leave it out,
But if it offer to thy nice survey
A spot, a stain, a blemish, or decay.
It not belongs to thee, the treacherous light
Or faithless stone abuse thy credulous sight.
Perhaps the magic of thy face, hath wrought
Upon th'enchanted Crystal, and so brought
Fantastic shadows to delude thine eyes
With airy repercussive sorceries,
Or else th'enamour'd Image pines away
For love of the fair Object, and so may
Wax pale and wan, and though the substance grow
Lively and fresh, that may consume with woe;

Give then no faith to the false specular stone,
But let thy beauties by th'effects be known.
Look (sweetest *Doris*) on my love-sick heart,
In that true mirror see how fair thou art.
There, by Love's never-erring Pencil drawn
Shalt thou behold thy face, like th'early dawn
Shoot through the shady covert of thy hair,
Enamelling, and perfuming the calm Air
With Pearls, and Roses, till thy Suns display
Their lids, and let out the imprison'd day;
Whilst Delphic Priests (enlight'ned by their Theme)
In amorous numbers court thy golden beam,
And from Love's Altars clouds of sighs arise
In smoking incense to adore thine eyes.
If then Love flow from Beauty, as th'effect,
How canst thou the resistless cause suspect?
Who would not brand that Fool, that should contend
There was no fire, where smoke and flames ascend?
Distrust is worse than scorn, not to believe
My harms, is greater wrong than not to grieve;
What cure can for my fest'ring sore be found,
Whilst thou believ'st thy beauty cannot wound?
Such humble thoughts more cruel Tyrants prove
Than all the pride that e'er usurp'd in Love,
For Beauty's Herald, here denounceth war,
There are false spies betray me to a snare.
If fire disguis'd in balls of snow were hurl'd
It unsuspected might consume the world;
Where our prevention ends, danger begins,
So Wolves in Sheep's, Lions in Asses' skins,
Might far more mischief work, because less fear'd,
Those, the whole flock, these, might kill all the herd.
Appear then as thou art, break through this cloud,
Confess thy beauty, though thou thence grow proud,
Be fair though scornful, rather let me find

Thee cruel, than thus mild, and more unkind;
Thy cruelty doth only me defy,
But these dull thoughts thee to thy self deny.
Whether thou mean to barter, or bestow
Thy self, 'tis fit thou thine own value know.
I will not cheat thee of thy self, nor pay
Less for thee than th'art worth, thou shalt not say
That is but brittle glass, which I have found
By strict enquiry a firm Diamond.
I'll trade with no such Indian fool who sells
Gold, Pearls, and precious stones, for Beads and Bells;
Nor will I take a present from your hand,
Which you or prize not, or not understand;
It not endears your bounty that I do
Esteem your gift, unless you do so too;
You undervalue me, when you bestow
On me, what you nor care for, nor yet know.
No (Lovely *Doris*) change thy thoughts, and be
In love first with thy self, and then with me.
You are afflicted that you are not fair,
And I as much tormented that you are,
What I admire, you scorn; what I love, hate,
Through different faiths, both share an equal Fate,
Fast to the truth, which you renounce, I stick,
I die a Martyr, you an Heretic.

To my friend *G. N.* from *Wrest*

I breathe (sweet *Ghib:*) the temperate air of *Wrest*
Where I no more with raging storms oppress'd,
Wear the cold nights out by the banks of Tweed,
On the bleak Mountains, where fierce tempests breed,
And everlasting Winter dwells; where mild

Favonius, and the Vernal winds, exil'd
Did never spread their wings: but the wild North
Brings sterile Fern, Thistles, and Brambles forth.
Here, steep'd in balmy dew, the pregnant Earth
Sends forth her teeming womb a flowery birth,
And cherish'd with the warm Sun's quick'ning heat,
Her porous bosom doth rich odours sweat;
Whose perfumes through the Ambient air diffuse
Such native Aromatics, as we use
No foreign Gums, nor essence fetch'd from far,
No Volatile spirits, nor compounds that are
Adulterate, but at Nature's cheap expense
With far more genuine sweets refresh the sense.
Such pure and uncompounded beauties, bless
This Mansion with an useful comeliness,
Devoid of Art: for here the Architect
Did not with curious skill a Pile erect
Of carved Marble, Touch, or Porphyry,
But built a house for hospitality;
No sumptuous Chimney-piece of shining stone
Invites the stranger's eye to gaze upon,
And coldly entertains his sight, but clear
And cheerful flames, cherish and warm him here:
No Doric, nor Corinthian Pillars grace
With Imagery this structure's naked face,
The Lord and Lady of this place delight
Rather to be in act, than seen in sight;
In stead of Statues, to adorn their wall
They throng with living men, their merry Hall,
Where, at large Tables fill'd with wholesome meats
The servant, Tenant, and kind neighbour eats.
Some of that rank, spun of a finer thread
Are with the Women, Steward, and Chaplain fed
With daintier cates; Others of better note
Whom wealth, parts, office, or the Herald's coat

Have sever'd from the common, freely sit
At the Lord's Table, whose spread sides admit
A large access of friends to fill those seats
Of his capacious circle, fill'd with meats
Of choicest relish, till his Oaken back
Under the load of pil'd-up dishes crack.
Nor think, because our Pyramids, and high
Exalted Turrets threaten not the sky,
That therefore *Wrest* of narrowness complains,
Or strait'ned Walls, for she more numerous trains
Of Noble guests daily receives, and those
Can with far more conveniency dispose
Than prouder Piles, where the vain builder spent
More cost in outward gay Embellishment
Than real use: which was the sole design
Of our contriver, who made things not fine,
But fit for service. *Amalthea's* Horn
Of plenty is not in Effigy worn,
Without the gate, but she within the door
Empties her free and unexhausted store.
Nor, crown'd with wheaten wreaths, doth *Ceres* stand
In stone, with a crook'd sickle in her hand:
Nor on a Marble Tun, his face besmear'd
With grapes, is curl'd unscissor'd *Bacchus* rear'd.
We offer not in Emblems to the eyes,
But to the taste, those useful Deities.
We press the juicy God, and quaff his blood,
And grind the Yellow Goddess into food.
Yet we decline not, all the work of Art,
But where more bounteous Nature bears a part
And guides her Hand-maid, if she but dispense
Fit matter, she with care and diligence
Employs her skill, for where the neighbour source
Powers forth her waters, she directs their course,
And entertains the flowing streams in deep

And spacious channels, where they slowly creep
In snaky windings, as the shelving ground
Leads them in circles, till they twice surround
This Island Mansion, which, i' th' centre placed,
Is with a double Crystal heaven embrac'd,
In which our watery constellations float,
Our Fishes, Swans, our Water-man and Boat,
Envy'd by those above, who wish to slake
Their star-burnt limbs, in our refreshing lake,
But they stick fast, nail'd to the barren Sphere,
Whilst our increase in fertile waters here
Disport, and wander freely where they please
Within the circuit of our narrow Seas.
    With various Trees we fringe the water's brink,
Whose thirsty roots the soaking moisture drink,
And whose extended boughs in equal ranks
Yield fruit, and shade, and beauty to the banks.
On this side young *Vertumnus* sits, and courts
His ruddy-cheek'd *Pomona*, *Zephyr* sports
On th'other, with lov'd Flora, yielding there
Sweets for the smell, sweets for the palate here.
But did you taste the high & mighty drink
Which from that Fountain flows, you'ld clearly think
The God of Wine did his plump clusters bring,
And crush the Falerne grape into our spring;
Or else disguis'd in watery Robes,did swim
To *Ceres* bed, and make her big of Him,
Begetting so himself on Her: for know
Our Vintage here in *March* doth nothing owe
To theirs in Autumn, but our fire boils here
As lusty liquor, as the Sun makes there.
    Thus I enjoy my self, and taste the fruit
Of this blest Peace, whilst toil'd in the pursuit
Of Bucks and Stags, th'emblem of war, you strive
To keep the memory of our Arms alive.

A New-year's gift
to the King

L ook back, old *Janus*, and survey
From Time's *birth* till this new-born day,
All the successful season bound
With Laurel wreaths, and Trophies crown'd;
Turn o'er the Annals past, and where
Happie auspicious days appear,
Mark'd with the whiter stone, that cast
On the dark brow of th'Ages past
A dazzling lustre, let them shine
In this succeeding circle's twine,
Till it be round with glories spread,
Then with it crown our *Charles* his head,
That we th'ensuing years may call
One great continued festival.
Fresh joys in varied forms apply,
To each distinct captivity.
Season his cares by day with nights
Crown'd with all conjugal delights,
May the choice beauties that enflame
His Royal breast be still the same,
And he still think them such, since more
Thou canst not give from Nature's store.
Then as a Father let him be
With numerous issue blest, and see
The fair and God-like off-spring grown
From budding stars to Suns full blown.
Circle with peaceful Olive boughs,
And conquering Bays, his Regal brows.
Let his strong virtues overcome,
And bring him bloodless Trophies home:
Strew all the pavements, where he treads

With loyal hearts, or Rebels' heads;
But, *Bifront*, open thou no more,
In his blest reign thy Temple door.

To the Queen

Thou great Commandress, that doest move
  Thy Sceptre o'er the Crown of Love,
And through his Empire, with the Awe
Of Thy chaste beams, doest give the Law,
From his profaner Altars, we
Turn to adore Thy Deity.
He, only can wild lust provoke,
Thou, those impurer flames canst choke;
And where he scatters looser fires,
Thou turn'st them into chaste desires:
His Kingdom knows no rule but this,
Whatever pleaseth, lawful is;
Thy sacred Lore shows us the path
Of Modesty, and constant Faith,
Which makes the rude Male satisfied
With one fair Female by his side;
Doth either sex to each unite,
And form Love's pure Hermaphrodite.
To this Thy faith, behold the wild
Satyr already reconciled,
Who from the influence of Thine eye
Hath suck'd the deep Divinity;
O free them then, that they may teach
The Centaur, and the Horseman preach
To Beasts and Birds, sweetly to rest
Each in his proper Lair and nest:
They shall convey it to the flood,

Till there Thy law be understood.
   So shall thou with thy pregnant fire
   The water, earth, and air, inspire.

To the New Year for the Countess of Carlisle

Give *Lucinda* Pearl, nor Stone,
   Lend them light who else have none,
Let Her beauty shine alone.

Gums nor spice bring from the East,
For the Phoenix in Her breast
Builds his funeral pile, and nest.

No attire thou canst invent,
Shall to grace her form be sent,
She adorns all ornament.

Give Her nothing, but restore
Those sweet smiles which heretofore
In Her cheerful eyes she wore.

Drive those envious clouds away,
Veils that have o'er-cast my day,
And eclips'd Her brighter ray.

Let the royal Goth mow down
This year's harvest with his own
Sword, and spare *Lucinda's* frown.

Janus, if when next I trace
Those sweet lines, I in her face
Read the Charter of my grace,

Then from bright *Apollo's* tree
Such a garland wreath'd shall be,
As shall Crown both Her and thee.

To my Honoured friend, Master Thomas May, upon his Comedy, *The Heir*

The *Heir* being born, was in his tender age
Rock'd in the Cradle of a private Stage,
Where lifted up by many a willing hand,
The child did from the first day fairly stand.
Since having gather'd strength, he dares prefer
His steps into the public Theatre
The World: where he despairs not but to find
A doom from men more able, not less kind;
  I but his Usher am, yet if my word
May pass, I dare be bound he will afford
Things must deserve a welcome, if well known,
Such as best writers would have wish'd their own.
  You shall observe his words in order meet,
And softly stealing on with equal feet
Slide into even numbers, with such grace
As each word had been moulded for that place.
  You shall perceive an amorous passion, spun
Into so smooth a web, as had the Sun
When he pursu'd the swiftly flying Maid,
Courted her in such language, she had stay'd.

A love so well express'd, must be the same
The Author felt himself from his fair flame.
  The whole Plot doth alike it self disclose
Through the five Acts, as doth the Lock that goes
With letters, for, till every one be known,
The Lock's as fast, as if you had found none.
And where his sportive Muse doth draw a thread
Of mirth, chaste Matrons may not blush to read.
  Thus have I thought it fitter to reveal
My want of art (dear friend) than to conceal
My love. It did appear I did not mean
So to commend thy well-wrought Comic-scene,
As men might judge my aim rather to be,
To gain praise to my self, than give it thee;
Though I can give thee none, but what thou hast
Deserv'd, and what must my faint breath out-last.
  Yet was this garment (though I skill-less be
To take thy measure) only made for thee,
And if it prove too scant, 'tis 'cause the stuff
Nature allow'd me was not large enough.

To my worthy friend Master Geo. Sands, on his translation of the Psalms

I press not to the choir, nor dare I greet
The holy place with my unhallow'd feet;
My unwash'd Muse, pollutes not things Divine,
Nor mingles her profaner notes with thine;
Here, humbly at the porch she stays,
And with glad ears sucks in thy sacred lays.
So, devout penitents of Old were wont,

Some without door, and some beneath the Font,
To stand and hear the Church's Liturgies,
Yet not assist the solemn exercise:
Sufficeth her, that she a lay-place gain,
To trim thy Vestments, or but bear thy train;
Though nor in tune, nor wing she reach thy Lark,
Her Lyric feet may dance before the Ark.
Who knows, but that her wand'ring eyes that run,
Now hunting Glow-worms, may adore the Sun,
A pure flame may, shot by Almighty power
Into her breast, the earthy flame devour.
My eyes,in penitential dew may steep
That brine, which they for sensual love did weep.
So (though 'gainst Nature's course) fire may be quench'd
With fire, and water be with water drench'd.
Perhaps my restless soul, tired with pursuit
Of mortal beauty, seeking without fruit
Contentment there, which hath not, when enjoy'd
Quench'd all her thirst, nor satisfi'd, though cloy'd,
Weary of her vain search below, Above
In the first Fair may find th'immortall Love.
Prompted by thy example then, no more
In moulds of clay will I my God adore;
But tear those Idols from my heart, and write
What his blest Spirit, not fond Love, shall indict;
Then, I no more shall court the verdant Bay,
But the dry leafless Trunk on *Golgotha*;
And rather strive to gain from thence one Thorn,
Than all the flourishing wreaths by Laureates worn.

To my much honoured friend,
Henry, Lord Cary of Lepington
on his translation of Malvezzi

My Lord,

In every trivial work 'tis known
Translators must be masters of their own,
And of their Author's language, but your task
A greater latitude of skill did ask.
For your *Malvezzi* first requir'd a man
To teach him speak vulgar Italian:
His matter's so sublime, so new his phrase
So far above the style of *Bembo's* days,
Old *Varchi's* rules, or what the *Crusca* yet
For current *Tuscan* mintage will admit,
As I believe your Marquess, by a good
Part of his Natives hardly understood.
You must expect no happier fate, 'tis true,
He is of noble birth, of nobler you:
So nor your thoughts, nor words fit common ears,
He writes, and you translate, both to your Peers.

To my worthy friend, M.
D'AVENANT, Upon his Excellent
Play, *The Just Italian*

I'll not mis-spend in praise, the narrow room
I borrow in this leafe; the Garlands bloom
From thine own seeds, that crown each glorious page
Of thy triumphant work; the sullen Age
Requires a Satire. What star guides the soul
Of these our froward times, that dare control,

Yet dare not learn to judge? When didst thou fly
From hence, clear candid Ingenuity?
I have beheld, when perch'd on the smooth brow
Of a fair modest troop, thou didst allow
Applause to slighter works; but then the weak
Spectator, gave the knowing leave to speak.
Now noise prevails, and he is tax'd for drouth
Of wit, that with the cry spends not his mouth.
Yet ask him, reason why he did not like;
Him, why he did; their ignorance will strike
Thy soul with scorn, and Pity: mark the places
Provoke their smiles, frowns, or distorted faces,
When, they admire, nod, shake the head: they'll be
A scene of mirth, a double Comedy.
But thy strong fancies (raptures of the brain,
Dress'd in Poetic flames) they entertain
As a bold, impious reach; for they'll still slight
All that exceeds Red Bull, and Cockpit flight.
These are the men in crowded heaps that throng
To that adulterate stage, where not a tongue
Of th'untuned Kennel, can a line repeat
Of serious sense: but like lips, meet like meat;
Whilst the true brood of Actors, that alone
Keep natural unstrain'd Action in her throne,
Behold their Benches bare, though they rehearse
The terser *Beaumonts* or great *Jonson's* verse.
Repine not Thou then, since this churlish fate
Rules not the stage alone; perhaps the State
Hath felt this rancour, where men great and good,
Have by the Rabble been misunderstood.
So was thy Play; whose clear, yet lofty strain,
Wise men, that govern Fate, shall entertain.

To the Reader of Master
William Davenant's
Play

It hath been said of old, that Plays be Feasts,
Poets the Cooks, and the Spectators Guests,
The Actors Waiters. From this Simile
Some have deriv'd an unsafe liberty,
To use their Judgments as their Tastes, which choose
Without control, this Dish, and that refuse:
But Wit allows not this large Privilege,
Either you must confess, or feel its edge;
Nor shall you make a current inference
If you transfer your reason to your sense:
Things are distinct, and must the same appear
To every piercing Eye, or well-tun'd ear.
Though sweets with yours, sharps best with my taste meet
Both must agree, this meat's, or sharp or sweet:
But if I scent a stench, or a perfume,
Whilst you smell nought at all, I may presume
You have that sense imperfect: So you may
Affect a sad, merry, or humorous Play,
If, though the kind distaste or please, the Good
And Bad, be by your Judgment understood;
But if, as in this Play, where with delight
I feast my Epicurean appetite,
With relishes so curious, as dispense
The utmost pleasure to the ravish'd sense,
You should profess that you can nothing meet
That hits your taste, either with sharp or sweet,
But cry out, 'tis insipid; your bold Tongue
May do its Master, not the Author wrong;
For men of better Palate will by it
Take the just elevation of your Wit.

To *Will. Davenant* my
Friend

When I behold, by warrant from thy Pen,
A Prince rigging our Fleets, arming our Men,
Conducting to remotest shores our force
(Without a *Dido* to retard his course)
And thence repelling in successful fight,
Th'usurping Foe (whose strength was all his Right)
By two brave *Heroes*, (whom we justly may
By *Homer's Ajax* or *Achilles* lay,)
I doubt the Author of the Tale of Troy,
With him, that makes his Fugitive enjoy
The Carthage Queen, and think thy Poem may
Impose upon Posterity, as they
Have done on us: What though Romances lie
Thus blended with more faithful History?
We, of th'adulterate mixture not complain,
But thence more Characters of Virtue gain;
More pregnant Patterns, of transcendent Worth,
Than barren and insipid Truth brings forth:
So oft the Bastard nobler fortune meets,
Than the dull Issue of the lawful sheets.

The Comparison

Dearest thy tresses are not threads of gold,
Nor thine eyes of Diamonds, nor do I hold
Thy lips for Rubies: Thy fair cheeks to be
Fresh Roses, nor thy teeth of Ivory:
The skin that doth thy dainty body sheathe
Not Alabaster is, nor dost thou breathe

Arabian odours, those the earth brings forth
Compar'd with which would but impair thy worth.
Such may be others' Mistresses, but mine
Holds nothing earthly, but is all divine.
Thy tresses are those rays that do arise
Not from one Sun, but two; Such are thy eyes:
Thy lips congealed Nectar are, and such
As but a Deity, there's none dare touch.
The perfect crimson that thy cheek doth clothe
(But only that it far excels them both)
Aurora's blush resembles, or that red
That *Iris* struts in when her mantle's spread.
Thy teeth in white do *Leda's* Swan exceed,
Thy skin's a heavenly and immortal weed,
And when thou breath'st, the winds are ready straight
To filch it from thee, and do therefore wait
Close at thy lips, and snatching it from thence
Bear it to heaven, where 'tis *Jove's* frankincense.
Fair Goddess, since thy feature makes thee one,
Yet be not such for these respects alone;
But as you are divine in outward view
So be within as fair, as good, as true.

The Compliment

O my dearest I shall grieve thee.
　　When I swear, yet sweet believe me,
By thine eyes, the tempting book
On which even crabbed old men look
I swear to thee (though none abhor them)
Yet I do not love thee for them.

I do not love thee for that fair,
Rich fan of thy most curious hair;
Though the wires thereof be drawn
Finer than the threads of lawn,
And are softer than the leaves
On which the subtle spinner weaves.

I do not love thee for those flowers
Growing on thy cheeks (love's bowers)
Though such cunning hath them spread,
None can part their white and red:
Love's golden arrows thence are shot,
Yet for them I love thee not.

I do not love thee for those soft,
Red coral lips I've kiss'd so oft;
Nor teeth of pearl, the double guard
To speech, whence music still is heard:
Though from those lips a kiss being taken
Would tyrants melt, and death awaken.

I do not love thee (O my fairest)
For that riches, for that rarest
Silver pillar which stands under
Thy round head, that globe of wonder;
Though that neck be whiter far;
Than towers of polish'd Ivory are.

I do not love thee for those mountains
Hill'd with snow, whence milky fountains,
(Sugar'd sweet, as syrup'd berries)
Must one day run, through pipes of cherries;
O how much those breasts do move me,
Yet for them I do not love thee:

I do not love thee for that belly,
Sleek as satin, soft as jelly,
Though within that Crystal round
Heaps of treasure might be found,
So rich, that for the least of them,
A King might leave his Diadem.

I do not love thee for those thighs,
Whose Alabaster rocks do rise
So high and even that they stand
Like Sea-marks to some happy land.
Happy are those eyes have seen them,
But happier they that sail between them.

I love thee not for thy moist palm,
Though the dew thereof be balm:
Nor for thy pretty leg and foot,
Although it be the precious root,
On which this goodly cedar grows,
(Sweet) I love thee not for those:

Nor for thy wit though pure and quick,
Whose substance no arithmetic
Can number down: nor for those charms
Mask'd in thy embracing arms;
Though in them one night to lie,
Dearest I would gladly die.

I love not for those eyes, nor hair,
Nor cheeks, nor lips, nor teeth so rare;
Nor for thy speech, thy neck, nor breast,
Nor for thy belly, nor the rest:
Nor for thy hand, nor foot so small,
But would'st thou know (dear sweet) for all.

On sight of a Gentlewoman's
face in the water

S tand still you floods, do not deface
    That Image which you bear:
So Votaries from every place,
    To you shall Altars rear.

No winds but Lovers' sighs blow here,
    To trouble these glad streams,
On which no star from any Sphere
    Did ever dart such beams.

To Crystal then in haste congeal,
    Lest you should lose your bliss:
And to my cruel fair reveal,
    How cold, how hard she is.

But if the envious *Nymphs* shall fear,
    Their beauties will be scorn'd,
And hire the ruder winds to tear
    That face which you adorn'd,

Then rage and foam amain, that we
    Their malice may despise:
When from your froth we soon shall see,
    A second *Venus* rise.

A Song

Ask me no more where *Jove* bestows,
When *June* is past, the fading rose:
For in your beauty's orient deep,
These flowers as in their causes, sleep.

Ask me no more, whither do stray
The golden Atoms of the day:
For in pure love heaven did prepare
Those powders to enrich your hair.

Ask me no more, whether doth hast,
The Nightingale when May is past:
For in your sweet dividing throat,
She winters and keeps warm her note.

Ask me no more, where those stars light,
That downwards fall in dead of night:
For in your eyes they sit, and there,
Fixed become, as in their sphere.

Ask me no more, if East or West,
The Phoenix builds her spicy nest:
For unto you at last she flies,
And in your fragrant bosom dies.

The Second Rapture

No, worldling, no, 'tis not thy gold,
  Which thou dost use but to behold;
Nor fortune, honour, nor long life,
Children, or friends, nor a good wife,
That makes thee happy; these things be
But shadows of felicity.
Give me a wench about thirteen,
Already voted to the Queen
Of lust and lovers, whose soft hair,
Fann'd with the breath of gentle air,
O'er spreads her shoulders like a tent,
And is her veil and ornament:
Whose tender touch, will make the blood
Wild in the aged, and the good;
Whose kisses fast'ned to the mouth
Of three-score years and longer slouth,
Renew the age, and whose bright eye
Obscures those lesser lights of sky:
Whose snowy breasts (if we may call
That snow, that never melts at all)
Makes *Jove* invent a new disguise,
In spite of *Juno's* jealousies;
Whose every part doth re-invite
The old decayed appetite:
And in whose sweet embraces I,
May melt my self to lust, and die.
  This is true bliss, and I confess,
  There is no other happiness.

The tinder

Of what mould did Nature frame me?
　　Or was it her intent to shame me,
That no woman can come near me,
Fair, but her I court to hear me?
Sure that mistress, to whose beauty
First I paid a lover's duty,
Burnt in rage my heart to tinder,
That nor prayers, nor tears can hinder,
But where ever I do turn me,
Every spark let fall doth burn me.
Women since you thus inflame me,
Flint and steel I'll ever name ye.

A Song

In her fair cheeks two pits do lie,
　　To bury those slain by her eye,
So spite of death, this comforts me,
That fairly buried I shall be.
My grave with rose and lily spread,
O 'tis a life to be so dead.
　　Come then and kill me with thy eye,
　　For if thou let me live, I die.

When I behold those lips again,
Reviving what those eyes have slain,
With kisses sweet, whose balsam pure,
Love's wounds as soon as made, can cure,
Me thinks 'tis sickness to be sound,
And there's no health to such a wound.

Come then, and kill me with thy eye,
For if thou let me live, I die.

When in her chaste breast I behold,
Those downy mounts of snow ne'er cold,
And those blest hearts her beauty kills,
Reviv'd by climbing those fair hilld
Me thinks there's life in such a death,
And so t' expire, inspires new breath.
   Come then, and kill me with thy eye,
   For if thou let me live, I die.

Nymph since no death is deadly where
Such choice of Antidotes are near,
And your keen eyes but kill in vain,
Those that are sound, as soon as slain,
That I no longer dead survive,
Your way's to bury me alive
In Cupid's cave, where happy I,
May dying live, and living die.
   Come then, and kill me with thy eye,
   For if thou let me live, I die.

To the Painter

Fond man, that hop'st to catch that face,
   With those false colours, whose short grace
Serves but to show the lookers-on,
The faults of thy presumption;
Or at the least to let us see,
That is divine, but yet not she:
Say you could imitate the rays,
Of those eyes that out-shine the days,

Or counterfeit in red and white,
That most uncounterfeited light
Of her complexion; yet canst thou,
(Great Master though thou be) tell how
To paint a Virtue? Then desist,
This fair your Artifice hath miss'd:
You should have mark'd how she begins,
To grow in virtue, not in sins:
Instead of that same rosy dye,
You should have drawn out modesty,
Whose beauty sits enthroned there,
And learn to look and blush at her.
Or can you colour just the same,
When virtue blushes or when shame:
When sickness, and when innocence,
Shows pale or white unto the sense?
Can such coarse varnish e'er be said
To imitate her white and red?
This may do well else-where in *Spain*,
Among those faces dyed in grain,
So you may thrive, and what you do,
Prove the best picture of the two.
Besides (if all I hear be true,)
'Tis taken ill by some that you
Should be so insolently vain,
As to contrive all that rich gain
Into one tablet, which alone
May teach us superstition;
Instructing our amazed eyes,
To admire and worship Imag'ries,
Such as quickly might outshine
Some new Saint, wer't allow'd a shrine,
And turn each wand'ring looker on
Into a new *Pygmalion.*
Yet your Art cannot equalise

This *Picture* in her lover's eyes;
His eyes the pencils are which limn
Her truly, as her's copy him,
His heart the Tablet which alone,
Is for that portrait the tru'st stone.
If you would a truer see,
Mark it in their posterity:
And you shall read it truly there,
When the glad world shall see their Heir.

Love's Courtship

Kiss lovely *Celia* and be kind,
Let my desires freedom find,
                    Sit thee down,
And we will make the Gods confess,
Mortals enjoy some happiness.

Mars would disdain his Mistress' charms
If he beheld thee in my arms,
                    And descend:
Thee his mortal Queen to make,
Or live as mortal for thy sake.

Venus must lose her title now,
And leave to brag of *Cupid's* bow,
                    Silly Queen.
She hath but one, but I can spy,
Ten thousand *Cupids* in thy eye.

Nor may the sun behold our bliss.
For sure thy eyes do dazzle his;
                    If thou fear

That he'll betray thee with his light,
Let me eclipse thee from his sight!

And while I shade thee from his eye,
Oh let me hear thee gently cry,
                    Celia yields.
Maids often lose their Maidenhead,
Ere they set foot in Nuptial bed.

On a Damask rose sticking upon a Lady's breast

Let pride grow big my rose, and let the clear
And damask colour of thy leaves appear.
Let scent and looks be sweet, and bless that hand,
That did transplant thee to thy sacred land.
O happy thou that in such garden rests,
That Paradise between a Lady's breasts.
There's an eternal spring; there shalt thou lie,
Betwixt two lily mounts, and never die.
There shalt thou spring amongst the fertile valleys,
By buds like thee that grow in 'midst of Alleys.
There none dare pluck thee, for that place is such.
That but a god divine, there's none dare touch,
If any but approach, straight doth arise
A blushing lightning flash, and blasts his eyes.
There, 'stead of rain, shall living fountains flow,
For wind her fragrant breath for ever blow.
Nor now, as erst, one Sun shall on thee shine,
But those two glorious suns, her eyes divine.
O then what Monarch would not think't a grace
To leave his Regal throne to have thy place.

My self, to gain thy blessed seat do vow.
Would be transform'd into a rose, as thou.

The protestation, a sonnet

No more shall meads be deck'd with flowers,
Nor sweetness dwell in rosy bowers:
Nor greenest buds on branches spring,
Nor warbling birds delight to sing,
Nor April violets paint the grove,
If I forsake my *Celia's* love.

The fish shall in the Ocean burn,
And fountains sweet shall bitter turn,
The humble oak no flood shall know,
When floods shall highest hills o'er-flow:
Black *Lethe* shall oblivion leave,
If e'er my *Celia* I deceive.

Love shall his bow and shaft lay by,
And *Venus'* doves want wings to fly:
The Sun refuse to show his light,
And day shall then be turn'd to night:
And in that night no star appear,
If once I leave my *Celia* dear.

Love shall no more inhabit earth,
Nor lovers more shall love for worth,
Nor joy above in heaven dwell,
Nor pain torment poor souls in hell;
Grim Death no more shall horrid prove:
If e'er I leave bright *Celia's* love.

The tooth-ache cured by a kiss

Fate's now grown merciful to men,
 Turning disease to bliss:
For had not kind Rheum vex'd me then,
 I might not *Celia* kiss.
Physicians you are now my scorn:
 For I have found a way
To cure diseases (when forlorn
 By your dull art) which may
Patch up a body for a time,
 But can restore to health,
No more than Chemists can sublime
 True Gold, the Indies' wealth.
That Angel sure, that us'd to move
 The pool men so admir'd,
Hath to her lip, the seat of love,
 As to his heaven, retired.

To his jealous Mistress

Admit (thou darling of mine eyes)
 I have some Idol lately fram'd,
That under such a false disguise,
 Our true loves might the less be fam'd.
  Canst thou, that knowest my heart suppose
  I'll fall from thee, and worship those?

Remember (dear) how loath and slow,
 I was to cast a look or smile,
Or one love-line to mis-bestow,
 Till thou hadst chang'd both face and style,

And art thou grown afraid to see,
  That mask put on, thou mad'st for me?

I dare not call those childish fears,
  Coming from love, much less from thee,
But wash away, with frequent tears,
  This counterfeit Idolatry,
    And henceforth kneel at ne'er a shrine,
    To blind the world, but only thine.

Additional Poems
from the 1642 Edition

On Mistress N. to the
green sickness

Stay coward blood, and do not yield
  To thy pale sister, beauty's field,
Who there displaying all her white
Ensigns, hath usurp'd thy right;
Invading thy peculiar throne,
The lip, where thou shouldst rule alone;
And on the cheek, where nature's care
Allotted each an equal share,
The spreading Lily only grows,
Whose milky deluge drowns thy Rose.
  Quit not the field faint blood, nor rush
In the short sally of a blush,
Upon thy sister foe, but strive
To keep an endless war alive;
Though peace do petty States maintain,
Here war alone makes beauty reign.

Upon a Mole in *Celia's*
Bosom

That lovely spot, which thou dost see
  In Celia's bosom was a Bee
Who built her amorous spicy nest
I'th' Hyblas of her either breast,
But from those Ivory Hives, she flew
To suck the Aromatic dew,
Which from the neighbour vale distils,
Which parts those two twin-sister hills.

There feasting on Ambrosial meat,
A rolling file of Balmy sweat,
(As in soft murmurs before death,
Swan-like she sung) chok'd up her breath,
So she in water did expire,
More precious than the Phoenix fire;
   Yet still her shadow there remains
Confin'd to those Elysian plains;
With this strict Law, that who shall lay
His bold lips on that milky way,
The sweet, and smart, from thence shall bring
Of the Bees Honey, and her sting.

An Hymeneal Song, on the Nuptials of the Lady *Ann Wentworth* and the Lord *Lovelace*

Break not the slumbers of the Bride,
But let the Sun in Triumph ride,
    Scattering his beamy light,

When she awakes, he shall resign
His rays: And she alone shall shine
    In glory all the night.

For she, till day return must keep
An Amorous Vigil, and not steep
Her fair eyes in the dew of sleep.

Yet gently whisper, as she lies,
And say her Lord waits her uprise,
        The Priests at the Altar stay,

With flowery wreaths the Virgin crew
Attend while some with roses strew,
        And Myrtles trim the way.

Now to the Temple, and the Priest,
See her convey'd, thence to the Feast;
Then back to bed, though not to rest:

For now, to crown his faith and truth,
We must admit the noble youth,
        To revel in Love's sphere;

To rule, as chief Intelligence
That Orb, and happy time dispense
        To wretched Lovers here.

For they're exalted far above
All hope, fear, change, or they do move
The wheel that spins the fates of Love.

They know no night, nor glaring noon,
Measure no hours of Sun or Moon,
        Nor mark Time's restless Glass:

Their kisses measure as they flow,
Minutes, and their embraces show
        The hours as they pass.

Their Motions, the year's Circle make,
And we from their conjunctions take
Rules to make Love an Almanac.

A Married Woman

When I shall marry, if I do not find
    A wife thus moulded, I'll create this mind:
Nor from her noble birth, nor ample dower,
Beauty, or wit, shall she derive a power
To prejudice my Right; but if she be
A subject born, she shall be so to me:
As to the soul the flesh, as Appetite
To Reason is, which shall our wills unite;
In habits so confirm'd, as no rough sway
Shall once appear, if she but learns t'obey.
For in habitual virtues, sense is wrought
To that calm temper, as the body's thought
To have nor blood, nor gall, if wild and rude
Passions of Lust, and Anger, are subdu'd;
When 'tis the fair obedience to the soul,
Doth in the birth those swelling Acts control.
If I in murder steep my furious rage,
Or with Adult'ry my hot lust assuage,
Will it suffice to say my sense, the Beast
Provoked me to't? could I my soul divest,
My plea were good, Lions, and bulls commit
Both freely, but man must in judgment sit,
And tame this Beast, for Adam was not free,
When in excuse he said, Eve gave it me:
Had he not eaten, she perhaps had been
Unpunish'd: his consent made hers a sin.

Love's Force

In the first ruder Age, when Love was wild,
Nor yet by Laws reclaim'd, not reconcil'd
To order, nor by Reason mann'd, but flew
Full-summ'd by Nature, on the instant view
Upon the wings of Appetite, at all
The eye could fair, or sense delightful call:
Election was not yet, but as their cheap
Food from the Oak, or the next Acorn-heap,
As water from the nearest spring or brook,
So men their undistinguish'd females took
By chance, not choice; but soon the heavenly spark
That in man's bosom lurk'd, broke through this dark
Confusion, then the noblest breast first felt
It self, for its own proper object melt.

A Fancy

Mark how this polish'd Eastern sheet
Doth with our Northern tincture meet,
For though the paper seem to sink,
Yet it receives, and bears the Ink;
And on her smooth soft brow these spots
Seem rather ornaments than blots;
Like those you Ladies use to place
Mysteriously about your face:
Not only to set off and break
Shadows and Eye beams, but to speak
To the skill'd Lover, and relate
Unheard, his sad or happy Fate:
Nor do their Characters delight,

As careless works of black and white:
But 'cause you underneath may find
A sense that can inform the mind;
Divine, or moral rules impart
Or Raptures of Poetic Art:
So what at first was only fit
To fold up silks, may wrap up wit.

Additional Poems
from the 1651 Edition

To his mistress

1.

G rieve not, my *Celia*, but with haste
Obey the fury of thy fate,
'Tis some perfection to waste
  Discreetly out our wretched state:
To be obedient in this sense,
Will prove thy virtue, though offence:

2.   Who knows but Destiny may relent,
  For many miracles have been,
Thou proving thus obedient
  To all the griefs she plunged thee in?
And then, the certainty she meant
Reverted is by accident.

3.   But yet I must confess 'tis much
  When we remember what hath been:
Thus parting never more to touch
  To let eternal absence in,
Though never was our pleasure yet
So pure, but chance distracted it.

4.   What, shall we then submit to fate,
  And die to one another's love?
No, *Celia*, no, my soul doth hate
  Those Lovers that inconstant prove,
Fate may be cruel, but if you decline,
The crime is yours, and all the glory mine.

Fate, and the Planets, sometimes bodies part,
But Canker'd nature only alters th'heart.

In praise of his Mistress

1.

Y ou that will a wonder know,
         Go with me!
Two suns in a heaven of snow
         Both burning be,
All they fire, that do but eye them,
But the snow's unmelted by them.

2.   Leaves of Crimson Tulips met
         Guide the way
Where two Pearly rows be set
         As white as day:
When they part themselves asunder
She breathes Oracles of wonder.

3.   Hills of Milk, with Azure mix'd
         Swell beneath,
Waving sweetly, yet still fix'd,
         While she doth breathe.
From those hills descends a valley,
Where all fall, that dare to dally.

4.   As fair Pillars under-stand
         Statues two,
Whiter than the Silver swan
         That swims in *Po*;
If at any time they move her
Every step begets a Lover.

5.   All this but the Casket is.
         Which contains

Such a Jewel, as the miss
        Breeds endless pains;
That's her mind, and they that know it
May admire, but cannot show it.

To *Celia*, on Love's
Ubiquity

As one that strives, being sick, and sick to death
   By changing places, to preserve a breath,
A tedious restless breath, removes and tries
A thousand rooms, a thousand policies,
To cozen pain, when he thinks to find ease,
At last he finds all change, but his disease,
So (like a Ball with fire and powder fill'd)
I restless am, yet live, each minute kill'd,
And with that moving torture must retain,
(With change of all things else) a constant pain.
Say I stay with you, presence is to me
Nought but a light, to show my misery,
And partings are as Racks, to plague love on,
The further stretch'd, the more affliction.
Go I to *Holland*, *France*, or farthest *Ind*,
I change but only Countries not my mind;
And though I pass through air and water free,
Despair and hopeless fate still follow me.
Whilst in the bosom of the waves I reel
My heart I'll liken to the tottering keel,
The sea to my own troubled fate, the wind
To your disdain, sent from a soul unkind:
But when I lift my sad looks to the skies,
Then shall I think I see my *Celia's* eyes,

And when a Cloud or storm appears between,
I shall remember what her frowns have been.
Thus, whatsoever course my fates allow,
All things but make me mind my business, you.
The good things that I meet I think streams be
From you, the fountain, but when bad I see,
How vile and cursed is that thing think I,
'That to such goodness is so contrary?
My whole life is 'bout you, the Centre Star,
But a perpetual Motion Circular:
I am the dial's hand, still walking round,
You are the Compass, and I never sound
Beyond your Circle, neither can I show
Aught, but what first expressed is in you:
Thus wheresoever my tears do cause me move
My fate still keeps me bounded with your love;
Which ere it die, or be extinct in me,
Time shall stand still, and moist waves flaming be.
Yet, being gone, think not on me, I am
A thing too wretched for thy thoughts to name;
But when I die, and wish all comforts given,
I'll think on you, and by you think on heaven.

Additional Poems
from Manuscripts

The Prologue to a Play
presented before the King and Queen, at an Entertainment of them by the Lord Chamberlain in Whitehall hall

Sir,
  Since you have pleased this night to unbend
Your serious thoughts, and with your Person lend
Your Palace out, and so are hither come
A stranger in your own house, not at home,
Divesting State, as if you meant alone
To make your Servants' loyal heart your Throne,
Oh see how wide those Values themselves display
To entertain his royal Guests, survey
What Arcs Triumphal, Statues, Altars, Shrines,
Inscrib'd to your great names, he these assigns;
So from that stock of Zeal, his Coarse Cates may
Borrow some relish though but thinly they
Cover'd his narrow Table, so may these
Succeeding trifles by that title please:
Else gracious Madam, must the influence
Of your fair Eyes propitious beams dispense
To Crown such pastimes as he could provide
To oil the lazy Minutes as they slide,
For well he knows upon your smiles depends
This night's Succes; since that alone Commends
All his endeavours, gives the Music praise
Painters and us, and gilds the Poet's bays.

The Epilogue to the same Play

Hunger is sharp, the Sated Stomach dull,
Feeding delights, 'twixt Emptiness and full:
The pleasure lies, not in the end, but streams
That flow betwixt two opposite Extremes.
So doth the flux from hot to cold Combine
An equal temper, such is noble wine
'Twixt fulsome Must and Vinegar too tart:
Pleasure's the scratching betwixt itch and smart,
It is a shifting Tartar, that still flies
From place to place, if it stand still it dies;
After much rest labour delights, when pain
Succeeds long travail, rest grows sweet again;
Pain is the base, on which his nimble feet
Move in continual change from sour to sweet.
   This the contriver of your sports tonight
Hath well observed, and so to fix delight
In a perpetual circle hath applied
The choicest objects that care could provide
To every sense. Only himself hath felt
The load of this great honour, and doth melt
All into humble thanks, and at your feet
Of both your Majesties prostrates the sweet
Perfume, of grateful service, which he swears
He will extend to such a length of years
As fits not us to tell, but doth belong
To a far abler pen, and nobler tongue.
Our task ends here, if we have hit the laws
Of true delight, his glad heart Joys, yet, 'cause
You cannot to succeeding pleasures climb
Till you grow weary of the instant time
He was Content this last piece should grow sour
Only to sweeten the Ensuing hour.

But if the Cook, Musician, Player, Poet,
Painter, and all, have fail'd, he'll make them know it
That have abused him, yet must grieve at this,
He should do Penance, when the Sin was his.

To M^rss Katherine Neville on her green sickness

White Innocence, that now lies spread,
　　Forsaken on thy widow'd bed,
Cold; and alone; if fear, love, hate,
Or shame recall thy crimson mate,
From his dark mazes, to reside
With thee his chaste and maiden bride,
Lest that he backward thence should flow
Congeal him with thy virgin snow:
But if his own heat, with thy pair
Of neighb'ring suns, and flaming hair,
Thaw him unto a new divorce,
Lest that from thee he take his course
O lodge me there, where I'll defeat
All future hopes of his retreat,
And force the fugitive to seek
A constant station in thy cheek.
So each shall have his proper place,
I in your heart, he in your face.

To his mistress retiring in affection

Fly not from him whose silent misery
  Breathes many an unwitness'd sigh to thee:
Who having felt thy scorn, yet constant is,
And whom, thy self, thou has call'd, only his.
When first mine eyes threw flames, whose spirit mov'd thee
Hadst thou not look'd again I had not lov'd thee.
Nature did ne'er two different things unite
With peace, which are by nature opposite.
If thou force nature, and be backward gone,
O blame not me, that strive to draw thee on:
But if my constant love shall fail to move thee,
Then know my reason hates thee, though I love thee.

To a Friend

Like to the hand that hath been used to play
  One lesson long, still runs the self-same way;
And waits not what the heavens bid it strike,
But doth presume by custom this will like;
So run my thoughts, which are so perfect grown,
So well acquainted with my passion,
That now they dare prevent me with their haste,
And ere I think to sigh, my sigh is past;
'Tis past, and flown to you, for you alone
Are all the object that I think upon;
And did not you supply my soul with thought
For want of action it to none were brought;
What though, our absent arms may not enfold
Real embraces, yet we firmly hold
Each other in possession; thus we see

The Lord enjoys his land, where e'er he be;
If Kings possess'd no more than where they sate,
What were they better than a mean estate?
This makes me firmly yours, you firmly mine,
That something, more than bodies, us combine.

A Lady's Prayer to Cupid

Since I must needs into thy school return,
 Be pitiful (O Love) and do not burn
Me with desire of cold and frozen Age,
Nor let me follow a fond boy or page:
But gentle Cupid give me if you can,
One to my love, whom I may call a man,
Of person comely, and of face as sweet,
Let him be sober, secret, and discreet,
Well practis'd in love's school, let him within
Wear all his beard, and none upon his chin.

Excuse of Absence

You'll ask, perhaps wherefore I stay,
 Loving so much, so long away,
O do not think 'twas I did part,
It was my body, not my heart,
For like a Compass in your love,
One foot is fix'd, and cannot move,
The other may follow her blind guide
Of giddy fortune, but not slide
Beyond your service, nor dares venture
To wander far from you the Centre.

On his Mistress looking in a glass

This flattering Glass whose smooth face wears
  Your shadow, where a sun appears
Was once a River of my tears.

About your cold heart they did make
A circle, where the briny lake
Congeal'd into a Crystal cake.

This Glass and shadow seem to say,
Like us the beauties you survey
Will quickly break or fly away.

Since then my tears can only show
You your own face, you cannot know
How fair you are, but by my woe.

Nor had the world else known your name
But that my sad verse spread the fame
Of thee, most fair and cruel dame.

Forsake but your disdainful mind
And in my song the world shall find
That you are not more fair than kind.

Change but your scorn, my verse shall chase
Decay far from you, and your face
Shall shine with an immortal grace.

Translations
from The Psalms

Psalme the first

1. Happy the man that doth not walk
    In wicked Counsels, nor hath lent
  His glad ear to the railing talk
    Of scorners, nor his prompt steps bent
    To wicked paths, where sinners went;

2. But to those safer tracts Confin'd,
    Which God's Law giving finger made,
  Never withdraws his Wearied mind
    From practice of that holy trade,
    By noon day's sun, or midnight's shade.

3. Like the Fair plant whom Neighbouring floods
    Refresh, whose leaf feels no decays,
  That not alone with flattering buds,
    But Early fruits his Lord's hope pays,
    So shall he thrive In all his ways.

4. But the loose sinner shall not share
    So fix'd a state; like the light dust
  That up and down the Empty Air
    The wild wind drives, with various Gust,
    So shall cross-fortunes toss the unJust.

5. Therefore, at the last Judgment day
    The trembling sinful Soul shall hide
  His Confused face, nor shall he stay
    Where the Elected Troops abide,
    But shall be chased far from their side.

6. For the Clear paths of Righteous men
    To the all seeing Lord are known,

But the dark maze and dismal den,
　　Where Sinners wander up and down
　　Shall by his hand be overthrown.

Psalm 2

1. 2.　　Why rage the heathen, wherefore swell
  3.　　　　The People with vain thoughts, why meet
Their Kings in Counsel to rebel
　　　　'Gainst God and Christ, trampling their sweet
　　　　But broken bonds under their feet?

4. 5.　　Alas the glorious God, that hath
　　　　　His throne in heaven, derides th' unsound
Plots of weak Mortals; in his wrath
　　　　Thus shall he speak, my self have crown'd
　　　　The Monarch of my holy ground.

7. 8.　　I will declare what God hath told;
　　　　　Thou art my son, this happy day
Did thy incarnate birth unfold;
　　　　Ask, and the heathen shall obey:
　　　　With the remotest Earth thy sway.'

9. 10.　Thy rod of Iron shall, if kings rise
  11.　　　　Against thee, bruise them into dust
Like pots of clay: therefore be wise
　　　　Ye Princes, and learn Judgments just,
　　　　Serve God with fear, Tremble, yet trust,

12.　　　Kiss and do homage to the Sun,
　　　　　Lest his displeasure ruin bring:
For if the fire be but begun,

Then happy those, that themselves fling
Under the Shelter of his wing.

Psalm 51

1.   Good God, unlock thy Magazines
     Of Mercy, and forgive my Sins.

2.   Oh, wash and purify the foul
     Pollution of my Sin-stain'd Soul.

3.   For I confess my faults, that lie
     In horrid shapes before mine Eye.

4.   Against thee only, and alone
     In thy sight was this evil done.
     That all Men might thy Justice see
     When thou art Judg'd for judging me.

5.   Even from my birth I did begin
     With mother's milk to Suck in Sin.

6.   But thou lov'st truth, and shalt impart
     Thy secret wisdom to my heart.

7.   Thou shalt with hysop purge me; so
     Shall I seem white as Mountain snow.

8.   Thou shalt send joyful news, and then
     My broken bones grow strong again.

9.   Let not thine Eyes my sins survey,
     But cast those Cancell'd debts away.

10.   Oh, make my Cleans'd heart, a pure Cell,
      Where a renewed Spirit may dwell.

11.   Cast me not from thy sight, nor chase
      Away from me thy Spirit of grace.

12.   Send me thy Saving health again,
      And with thy Spirit those Joys maintain.

13.   Then will I preach thy ways, and draw
      Converted Sinners to Thy law.

14. 15.   Oh God my God of health, unseal
          My blood-shut lips, and I'll reveal
          What mercies in thy Justice dwell,
          And with loud Voice thy Praises tell.

16. 17.   Could Sacrifice have purged my vice
          Lord,I had brought thee Sacrifice:
          But though burnt offerings are refus'd
          Thou shalt accept the heart that's bruis'd
          The humbled Soul, the spirit oppress'd.
          Lord such oblations please thee best.

18.   Bless Sion lord, repair with pity
      The ruins of thy holy City.

19.   Then will we holy dower present thee,
      And peace offerings that Content thee,
      And then thine Altars shall be press'd
      With many a Sacrificed beast.

Psalm 91

1. 2.   Make the great God thy Fort, and dwell
    3.   In him by Faith and do not Care
        (So shaded) for the power of hell,
            Or for the Cunning Fowler's snare,
            Or poison of th'infected Air.

4. 5.   His plumes shall make a downy bed,
            Where thou shalt rest, he shall display
        His wings of truth over thy head,
            Which like a shield shall drive away
            The fears of night, the darts of day.

6. 7.   The winged plague that flies by night,
            The murdering sword that kills by day,
        Shall not thy peaceful sleeps affright,
            Though on thy right and left hand they
            A thousand and ten thousand slay.

9. 10.   Yet shall thine Eyes behold the fall
            Of Sinners, but, because thy heart
        Dwells with the Lord, not one of all
            Those ills, nor yet the plaguey dart.
            Shall dare approach near where thou art.

11. 13.   His Angels shall direct thy legs
            And guard them in the Stony street;
        On Lions' whelps and Adders' eggs
            Thy Steps shall March, and if thou meet
            With Dragons, they shall kiss thy feet.

14. 15.   When thou art troubled, he shall hear,
    16.   And help thee, for thy Love embraced
    And knew his name, Therefore he'll rear

Thy honours high, and when thou hast
Enjoy'd them long, Save thee at last.

Psalm 104

1. My Soul the great God's praises sings
   Encircled round with glory's wings;

2. Clothed with light, o'er whom the Sky
   Hangs like a Starry Canopy:

3. Who dwells upon the gliding streams,
   Enamel'd with his golden beams;
   Enthron'd in Clouds as in a Chair,
   He rides in triumph through the air:

4. The winds and flaming Element
   Are on His great Ambassage sent.

5. The Fabric of the Earth shall stand
   For aye, built by his powerful hand.

6. 7. The floods, that with their wat'ry robe
8. 9. Once cover'd all this Earthly Globe,
   (Soon as thy thundering Voice was heard,)
   Fled fast, and straight the hills appear'd.
   The humble Valleys saw the Sun,
   Whilst the affrighted waters run
   Into their Channels, and no more
   Shall drown the Earth, or pass the shore.

10. Along those vales the Cool Springs flow,
    And wash the Mountains' feet below.

11.   Hither for Drink, the whole herd strays,
        There the wild Ass, his Thirst allays;

12.   And on the Boughs that shade the spring
        The feather'd choir shall sit and sing.

13. 14. When on her womb thy dew is shed
    15. The pregnant Earth is brought to bed,
        And with a fruitful birth increas'd
        Yields herbs and grass for Man and beast,
        Heart-strengthening bread, Care-drowning wine,
        And oil, that makes the sleek face shine.

16.   On Lebanon his Cedars stand:
        Trees full of Sap, works of his hand;

17.   In them the Birds their Cabins dight,
        The Fir tree is the Stork's delight,

18.   The wild Goat on the hills, in Cells
        Of Rock, the hermit, Coney, dwells.

19.   The Moon observes her Course, the Sun
        Knows when his weary race is done:

20.   And when the night her dark veil spreads
        The wilder beasts forsake their sheds;

21.   The hungry Lions hunt for blood,
        And roaring beg from God their food.

22. 23. The Sun returns, these beasts of prey
        Fly to their Dens, and from the day;
        And whilst they in dark Caverns lurk,
        Man till the evening goes to work.

24.   How full of Creatures is the Earth,
            To which thy wisdom gave their birth!

25.   And those that in the wide Sea breed
            The bounds of number far exceed:

26.   There the huge whales with finny feet
            Dance underneath the Sailing fleet.

27. 28. All these expect their nourishment
29. 30. From thee, and gather what is Sent.
            Be thy hand open, they are fed:
            Be thy face hid, astonished.
            If thou withdraw their Soul, they must
            Return unto their former dust.
            If thou send back thy breath the face
            Of the Earth, is spread with a new race.

31.   God's glory shall for ever stay,
            He shall with joy his works survey.

32. 33. The steadfast Earth shall shake, if he
            Look down, & if the Mountains be
            Touch'd, they shall smoke. Yet still my verse
            Shall whilst I live his praise rehearse;

34.   In him with joy my thoughts shall meet,
            He makes my Meditations sweet.

35.   The Sinner shall appear no more.
            Then oh my Soul, thy Lord adore.

Psalm 113

1. 2.   Ye Children of the Lord, that wait
    3.   Upon His will, sing Hymns divine
From henceforth, to time's endless date
        To his name prais'd, from the first shine
        Of th'Early Sun, till it decline.

4, 5.   The hosts of Heaven, or Earth have none
    6.   May to his height of glory rise;
For who like him hath fix'd his Throne
        So high, yet bends down to the skies
        And lower Earth his humble Eyes?

7. 8.   The poor from loathed Dust he draws,
    9.   And makes them regal state invest
'Mongst kings, that gives his People Laws:
        He makes the barren Mother rest
        Under her roof, with Children blest.

Psalm 114

1. 2.   When the seed of Jacob fled
        From the cruel Pharaoh's land,
Judah was in Safety led
        By the Lord, whose powerful hand
        Guided all the Hebrew band.

3. 4.   This the Sea saw, and dismay'd
        Flies, swift Jordan backward makes,
Mountains skipp'd like rams afraid,
        And the lower hillocks shakes
        Like a tender Lamb that quakes.

5. 6.	What oh Sea, hath thee dismay'd?

5. 6.   What oh Sea, hath thee dismay'd?
          Why did Jordan backwards make?
          Mountains why, like rams afraid,
          Skipp'd ye, wherefore did ye shake
          Hillocks, like the lambs that quake?

7. 8.   Tremble oh thou steadfast Earth
              At the presence of the Lord
          That makes rocks give Rivers birth,
              And by virtue of whose word
          Flints shall flowing springs afford.

Psalm 119
BEATI IMMACULATI. 1ST

Aleph:

1.   Blest is he that Spotless stands
       In the way of God's commands.

2.   Blessed he that keeps his word,
       Whose entire heart seeks the Lord:

3.   For the Man that walketh in
       His just paths, Commits no Sin.

4.   By thy strict Commands we are
       Bound to keep thy Laws with care,

5.   Oh that my steps might not slide
       From thy Statutes' perfect guide.

6.   So shall I decline thy wrath
       Treading thy Commanded path;

7.   Having learn'd thy righteous ways
    With true heart I'll sing thy praise;

8.   In thy Statutes I'll persever,
    Then forsake me not for ever!

IN QUO CORRIGET. 2.

Beth.

9.   How shall youth but by the level
    Of thy word be kept from evil?

10.   Let my soul that seeks the way
    Of thy truth not go astray;

11.   Where lest my frail Feet might slide
    In my heart thy words I hide.

12.   Blest be thou oh Lord, oh show
    How I may thy statutes know.

13.   I have publish'd the divine
    Judgments of thy mouth with mine,

14.   Which have fill'd my soul with pleasure
    More than all the heaps of treasure.

15.   They shall all the Subject prove
    Of my talk, and of my love;

16.   Those my darlings no time shall
    From my Memory let fall.

Retribue servo tuo. 3.

Gimel:

17.   Let Thy grace, Lord, preserve me,
        That I may but live to serve thee;

18.   Open my dark Eyes that I
        May thy wonderous laws descry;

19.   Let thy glorious light appear:
        I am but a pilgrim here,

20.   Yet the zeal of their desire
        Hath even set my heart on fire.

21.   Thy fierce rod and curse o'er taketh
        Him that proudly thee forsaketh:

22.   I have kept thy laws oh God,
        Turn from me thy curse and rod.

23.   Though combined Princes rail'd,
        Yet thy Servant hath not fail'd

24.   In their Study to abide,
        For they are my joy, my guide.

Adhæsit pavimento. 4.

Daleth:

25.   For thy word's sake, give new birth
        To my soul that Cleaves to Earth.

26.   Thou hast heard my Tongue untwine
        All my ways, Lord teach me Thine.

27.   Make me know them that I may
       All thy wondrous works display.

28.   Thou hast said the word, then bring
       Ease to my Soul languishing.

29.   Plant in me, thy Laws' true Love
       And the veil of Lies remove.

30.   I have chosen truth to Lie
       The fix'd object of mine Eye.

31.   On thy word my faith I grounded,
       Let me not then be confounded.

32.   When my Soul from bonds is freed,
       I shall run thy ways with speed.

LEGEM PONE. 5.

HE.

33.   Teach me Lord, thy ways, and I
       From that road will never fly.

34.   Give me knowledge,that I may
       With my heart, thy laws obey.

35.   Unto that Path, my steps move,
       For I there have fix'd my love.

36.   Fill my heart with those pure fires,
       Not with Covetous desires.

37.   To vain sights Lord let me be
       Blind, but thy ways let me see.

38.   Make Thy promise firm to me
        That with fear have served thee.

39.   'Cause thy Judgments ever were
        Sweet divert the shame I fear.

40.   Let not him in Justice perish
        That desires, thy Laws to cherish.

            ET VENIAT SUPER ME. 6.
VAU:
41.   Let thy Loving Mercies cure me,
        As thy promises assure me,

42.   So shall the Blasphemers see
        I not vainly trust in thee;

43.   Take not quite the words away
        Of thy truth, that are my stay,

44.   Then I'll keep thy laws, even till
        Winged time it self stand still;

45.   And whilst I pursue thy search,
        With secure steps will I march.

46.   Unashamed I'll record,
        Even before great kings thy word.

47.   That shall be my joy, for there
        My thoughts ever fixed were.

48.   With bent mind and stretch'd-out hands
        I will seek thy lov'd commands.

ZAINE:

49.   Think upon thy promise made,
For in that my trust is laid,

50.   That my Comfort in distress,
That hath brought my life redress.

51.   Though the proud hath scorn'd me, they
Make me not forsake thy way;

52.   Thy eternal Judgments brought
Joy, to my rememb'ring thought;

53.   With great Sorrow I am taken
When I see thy laws forsaken:

54.   Which have made me songs of mirth
In this pilgrimage of Earth;

55.   Which I mindful was to keep,
When I had forgot to sleep.

56.   Thy Commands I did embrace,
Therefore I obtain'd Thy grace.

PORTIO MEA, DOMINE. 8.

HETH:

57.   Thou o Lord, art my reward,
To thy laws my thoughts are squar'd.

58.   With an humble heart I crave
Thou wilt promis'd mercy have.

59.   I have mark'd my steps, and now
        To thy ways my feet I bow.

60.   Nor have I the time delay'd,
        But with haste this Journey made,

61.   Where though bands of sinners lay
        Snaring nets, I keep my way.

62.   I my self at Midnight raise,
        Singing thy just Judgments' praise.

63.   I converse with those that bear
        To thy laws obedient fear.

64.   Teach me them, Lord, by that grace
        Which hath fill'd the world's wide space.

Psalm 137

1.   Sitting by the streams that Glide
        Down by Babel's Tow'ring wall,
   With our tears we fill'd the tide
        Whilst our Mindful thoughts recall
        Thee Oh Sion, and thy fall.

2.   Our neglected harps unstrung,
        Not acquainted with the hand
   Of the skilful Tuner, hung
        On the willow trees that stand
        Planted in the Neighbour land.

3.   Yet the spiteful foe Commands
        Songs of Mirth, and bids us lay
    To dumb harps, our Captive hands,
        And, (to scoff our sorrows) say,
        Sing us some sweet hebrew lay.

4.   But, say we, our holy strain
        Is too pure for heathen land,
    Nor may we god's Hymns profane,
        Or move either voice or hand
        To delight a savage band.

5.   Holy Salem if thy love
        Fall from my forgetful heart,
    My the skill by which I move
        Strings of Music tun'd with art,
        From my wither'd hand depart.

6.   May my speechless tongue give sound
        To no accents, but remain
    To my prison Roof fast bound,
        If my sad soul Entertain
        Mirth, till thou rejoice again!

7.   In that day remember, Lord
        Edom's brood, that in our groans
    They Triumph; and with fire and sword
        Burn their City, hew their bones.
        And make all One heap of stones.

8.   Cruel Babel, thou shalt feel
        The Revenger of our groans,
    When the happy Victor's steel
        As thine, ours, shall hew thy bones,
        And make thee one heap of stones.

9.   Men shall bless the hand that tears
           From the Mothers' soft embrace
     Sucking Infants, and besmears
           With their brains, the Rugged faces
           Of the Rocks and stony places.

Notes

General:
The word "mistress" (or "mistris") occurs frequently in the poems printed in this volume, as it does in many poems of the era. No sexual relationship is necessarily implied by this word in Carew's time. The woman in question is most likely to be simply the object of affection or admiration.

p.21 A Beautiful Mistress
Set to music by Lawes and published in *Ayres and Dialogues* (1653).

p.26 Secrecy Protested
Set to music by Lawes; *Ayres and Dialogues* (1655 edition)

p.28 Good counsel to a young maid
calenture : (a) a kind of sunstroke, or, at least, delirium occasioned by overlong exposure to extreme heat; or, (b) a fever.

p30-31, To my inconstant Mistress
First and third stanzas set by Lawes (1653).

p.33 Ingrateful beauty threatened
imp'd : a word from falconry, which describes the process whereby a new feather is grafted onto, and grows from, an old broken one. No longer in use, the word was popular with poets of the 16th and 17th centuries..

p.34 A Looking Glass.
The version in the Harleian manuscript (Harl. 6057 f.8 in the British Library—"a quarto verse miscellany, largely in a single professional hand, with later additions... in three of four other hands, 65 leaves... Compiled by one Thomas Crosse")[1] differs considerably from the version printed here, and is as follows:

> This flattering glass, whose smooth face wears
> Your shadow, which a sun appears,
> Was once a river of my tears,

---

1 http://www.celm-ms.org.uk/repositories/british-library-harley-6000.html. Accessed 21 November 2015.

About your cold heart they did make
A circle, where the briny lake
Congeal'd into a crystal cake.

This glass and shadow seem to say,
Like us, the beauties you survey
Will quickly break, or fly away.

Since then my tears can only show
You your own face, you cannot know
How fair you are, but by my woe.

Nor had the world else known your name,
But that my sad verse spread the fame
Of thee, most fair and cruel dame!

Forsake but your disdainful mind,
And in my songs the world shall find
That you are not more fair than kind.

Change but your scorn: my verse shall chase
Decay far from you, and your face
Shall shine with an immortal grace.

p.35 An Elegy on the La. Pen.
The Lady of the title was Martha Temple, daughter of Sir Thomas
Temple. Martha married Sir Thomas Peniston, and died in January
1620.

p.43-45 To Saxham
Saxham Parva was the family seat of the Crofts, whose third son, John,
was one of Carew's closest friends, and whom he met while in the
Ambassador's retinue in France. One of John's sisters married Thomas
Killigrew. Commendatory poems on country houses were a feature of
the period, with Jonson having composed a significant example of the
genre in 'To Penshurst'.

— p.44. *Volary* : aviary

p.45 *Ribband* : ribbon

p.46 To the King, at his entrance into Saxham
King James I often visited Saxham. As the title indicates, this would have been composed by Carew for his friend John to read to the visiting monarch.

p48. Upon the sickness of (E.S.)
Dian : Diana, Roman goddess of the hunt, the moon and childbirth.
Votaress : priestess.
Hymen : Greek god of marriage ceremonies

p.49 A New Year's Sacrifice / To Lucinda
Lucinda was Lucy Percy, daughter of the Earl of Northumberland and second wife of James Hay, Earl of Carlisle, whom she wed in 1617. She was a famous beauty, whose charms were also celebrated in verse by Herrick and Waller, as well as in a more risqué poem by Suckling, which takes the form of a dialogue between "T.C." and the author. T.C. is assumed to be Carew, given that the two poets were close.

p.50 *Delphic fire* : In the temple of Apollo at Delphi, an eternal flame burned.

p.55 *phaeton*: here a carriage or chariot, but in the Greek myth, Phaeton was actually the son of the oceanid, Clymene, and Apollo, the sun god. Young Phaeton boasted of his lineage to his friends; when they mocked him, he sought to prove it and asked his father for some proof of his relationship with the sun. Accordingly he was given control of the sun chariot for a day. Alas for Phaeton, he lost control of the horses, and to save the Earth from being burned, Zeus was forced to kill him with a thunderbolt.

p.58 In the person of a Lady
Set by Lawes, *Ayres and Dialogues* (1653)

pp.63-65 A Pastoral Dialogue
Set by Lawes, *Ayres and Dialogues* (1653)

p.65 To my Cousin (C.R.) marrying my Lady (A.)
The persons in the title are thought to be Carew Ralegh, second son of the poet Sir Walter Ralegh, who wed Philippa, the widow of Sir Antony Ashley (and thus Lady A.). Carew's and Ralegh's relationship

was much more distant than that of cousins, but it was not uncommon to address distant relations with this epithet.

— p.66 *Hymeneal rite*: wedding celebration
— *Semele*: a priestess of Zeus, who attracted the god's attention as she sacrificed a bull at the altar. He become besotted with her and began to visit her in disguise. His affair with Semele was discovered by Hera, Zeus' wife, who decided to nip matters in the bud. She appeared to Semele disguised as an old woman; when Semele told her that her lover was actually Zeus, Hera suggested that she insist on proof of this. Despite Zeus begging her not to demand this of him, he was forced to appear in all his glory to prove his identity; even though he dampened things down as far as he could, Semele was still consumed by the fires from his lightning bolts.

p.66 A Lover upon an Accident...
Set by Lawes, *Ayres and Dialogues* (1655)

p.67-72 A Rapture
Perhaps Carew's most famous poem, and also his longest, this in many ways made his reputation and also caused him some notoriety.

— p67 *Masquer* : actor in a masque.
— p67 *Colossus* (of Rhodes) : one of the wonders of the ancient world, the Colossus was a statue of a man that bestrode the entrance to the island's harbour.
— p69 *Apennine* : the Apennine mountains stretch the length of Italy.
— *Eglantine*: a kind of rose also known as sweetbriar.
— *Alembic* : a distillation vessel used by alchemists, the alembic consisted of two separate parts connected by a tube. Similar to a retort.

— p70 *Danae* : only child of King Acrisius or Argos, and Queen Eurydice. Having no male heir, Acrisius went to Delphi to ask if things would change for the better. he was told that he would have no son but that his daughter would, but that he himself would be killed by his grandson. Danae had had no children at his point, and Acrisius sought to protect himself by shutting her in a bronze chamber beneath his palace's courtyard. Beyond all human sight, she was not beyond the sight of the gods however, and she caught the eye of Zeus, who came to her in the form of golden rain through the roof of the chamber.

She bore a son as a result of this encounter, Perseus, later a great hero. Frightened by what had happened, Acrisius had mother and child thrown into the sea, but Posiedon calmed the waves at the request of Zeus, and mother and son survived, washed up on the shores of the island of Seriphos, where they were rescued by Dictys, brother of King Polydectes. Danae resisted the King's attentions and he agreed to leave her alone if Perseus would only bring him the hear of the gorgon, Medusa. This he did, rescuing Andromeda in the process. Afterwards, visiting Larissa, where athletic Games were being held, Perseus threw a javelin which struck the aged Acrisius by accident, killing him, and thus proving the truth of the prediction.

— *Cyprian* (200-258) : Carthaginian bishop and significant early Christian writer.

— *Roman Lucrece* : Lucretia, a legendary Roman woman, whose fate is bound up with the foundation of the Roman republic. Lucretia was abducted and raped by the son of an Etruscan king, and thereafter committed suicide. This was a trigger for the overthrow of the Roman monarchy and the establishment of the republic. The story was the subject of Shakespeare's long poem, *The Rape of Lucrece* (1594).

— *Aretine* : Pietro Aretino (1492-1556, born in Arezzo, hence the name Aretino, meaning "of Arezzo"). Famous for a group of sonnets composed for some drawings by the mannerist painter, Giulio Romano.

— *Lais* : Lais of Corinth, a famed courtesan from the late 5th century BC. She was said to be the most beautiful woman of her time.

— p71 *Ithaca* : Greek island, home of Odysseus.

— *Daphne* : a naiad (water-nymph) in Greek mythology. Pursued by Apollo, she resisted his advances. She pleaded with her father, the river-god Ladon, to help her and he turned her into a laurel tree. Therefater the winner of the Pythian games in Delphi, held every four years, was awarded a laurel wreath, to commemorate Apollo's love for Daphne.

— *Delphic lyre* : Apollo's instrument.

— *Laura* : the unattainable beloved of *Petrarch* (Francesco Petrarca, 1304-1374), a woman he glimpsed in a church in Avignon in 1327.

Laura was married, and quite properly (for the time) refused to speak to the poet. She is in many ways the ancestral stereotype for all subsequent unattainable women in lyric poetry.

— p72 *maugre* : meagre.

p72 Epitaph on the Lady Mary Villiers
The Lady Villiers of the title is a mystery. The one Lady Villiers we know of who was also known to Carew lived to a ripe old age.

p74 Epitaph on the Lady S
Probably Lady Mary Salter, wife of Sir William Salter, the latter also being a Courtier, in this case bearing the position of Carver-in-Ordinary. Lady Mary died in 1631 at the age of 30.

— *Chrysolite* : a precious stone, green in colour.

— *Aaron's Ephod* : an ephod was a priestly vestment in the Jewish religion. In the Bible most mentions of it explain that it is made of linen. Aaron was the older brother of Moses., and first High Priest of the Israelites.

p75 Maria Wentworth
cherubin : cherub, little angel. (N.B. the plural form is *cherubim*.)

p76 On the Tomb of the Duke of Buckingham
Buckingham, a favourite of King James I, was murdered in 1628 by John Felton, who stabbed him in the Greyhound Inn, Portsmouth, where the Duke was lodging. Felton was a Lieutenant in the Army who had suffered in combat and had not received promotions that he thought were his due. He evidently thought that, given the enormous unpopularity of the Duke following a bungled military expedition to France, the assassination would be welcomed. So it was, by a large proportion of the general public, but, alas for Felton, the authorities took a more stringent – and it must be said, legal – view. He was tried and hanged for the murder.

— *two kings rais'd* : Buckingham was a favourite of James I, and was also well-regarded, and indeed protected, by Charles I.

p79 Four Songs
The play from which these songs are drawn is unknown, and is presumed lost. According to Arthur Vincent, editor of the Muse's Library edition of Carew's work, the author's friend, Thomas Killigrew "introduced the first song, 'Of Jealousy', into his play *Cicilia and Clorinda* (Part II. Act V. sc. ii.), written at Florence in 1651, and added the following note:

> 'This chorus was written by Mr. Thomas Carew, cupbearer to Charles I., and sung in a Masque at Whitehall 1633. And I presume to make use of it here, because in the first design, 'twas writ at my request upon a dispute held between Mistress Cecilia Crofts and myself, when he was present; she being then a maid-of-honour. This I have set down, lest any man should believe me so foolish as to steal such a poem from so famous an author; or so vain as to pretend to the making of it myself; and those that are not satisfied with this apology, and this song in this place, I am always ready to give them a worse of my own.'"

Killigrew married Cecilia Crofts.

p80 On Feminine Honour
Cultures (or *culters*) : ploughshares

p85 To Ben Jonson
Jonson's play, *The New Inn*, was first given in January 1630 and was booed off before the premiere performance was finished. This poem is one of several published by Jonson's supporters, of whom Carew was one of the most prominent.

— *Alchemist* : Jonson's play, *The Alchemist* (1610).

— *Gavel-kind* : likely refers to the Judge's gavel, rapped at the time of sentencing.

—p86 *Goodwin* : refers to Goodwin Sands, quicksands off the Kent coast.

p87 Obsequies to the Lady Anne Hay
The Lady in question was the daughter of the Earl of Carlisle and Lady

Honora, née Denny, daughter of Sir Edward Denny, Earl of Norwich. Carew was distantly related to Lady Carlisle.

—p88 *Apelles* : Greek painter of the 4th century BC. No works survive but it has been suggested that a mural of Venus, and a mosaic of the Battle of Issus, found in Pompeii, are copies of Apellean originals. This is *possible,* if not likely, as a number of his works were taken to Rome and put on public display there.

— *Katherine or Clare* : Clare refers to the Order of Saint Clare (commonly known as the "Poor Clares", an order of nuns dating back to the 13th century and founded by St Clare of Assisi and St Francis of Assisi. Katherine is likely to refer to St Catherine of Siena (1347-1380), of the Tertiary Dominican order.

p88 To the Countess of Anglesey
The Countess was born Elizabeth Sheldon, of Leicester, and married Christopher Villiers, younger brother of the Duke of Buckingham. Villiers was made Earl of Anglesey in 1623, and died in 1630.

— *Æson* : in Greek mythology the son of Cretheus and Tyro and father of Jason (he of the Argonauts). One of the myths has Medea, Jason's wife, slitting Æson's throat and putting his corpse in a cauldron; Æson was them reborn as a young man. She offered to the daughters of Pelias, Æson's enemy, to do the same for their father, but then declined to raise him from the dead.
    The reference to a "bath" concerns the potion in which he was laid in the cauldron, which had revivifying powers.

— p91 *Juno* : Queen of the Gods in Roman mythology.

— p92 *Buckingham* : The Countess' brother-in-law.

p.92 An Elegy upon the death of Donne
First published, with several elegiac poems in memory of Donne by several hands, in Donne's posthumous *Poems,* 1633. Carew was a great admirer of Donne, and the latter's influence on Carew's work is marked.

— p93 *Delphic* : refers to the Oracle at Delphi.

— *Promethean* : refers to Prometheus, the Titan, who, in Greek mythology, was the creator of the human race, and who gave it the gift of fire, which he had stolen from Mount Olympus.

— *Anacreon* : one of the nine canonical lyric poets of Ancient Greece, he was active in the 6th century BC. He was Ionian, and wrote in the Ionic dialect of Greek. After his death, a statue of Anacreon was erected in the Acropolis, but this is no longer extant.

— *Pindar* : another of the canonical nine lyric poets, Pindar was active in the 5th century BC. He is particularly famous in modern times for his Odes in honour of famous men, and Olympic victors.

— *Orpheus* : poet and musician in Ancient Greek myth, born in Thrace, legendary for both his art, and for his supposed descent into the underworld, attempting to rescue his wife, Eurydice. Throughout the Classical era, he was regarded as the great progenitor of all Greek poetry. The myth was probably known to Carew through the works of the Roman poet, Ovid, who – along with many other early retellers of the story – emphasises Orpheus' love for young boys.

p95 In Answer of an Elegiacal Letter from Aurelian Townsend
Townsend was a poet and writer of masques for the Court. He had been in the retinue of Lord Herbert of Cherbury on his embassy to France in 1608, and was esteemed for his linguistic skills.

— *Barbican* : where Townsend lived.

— *Gustavus Adolphus* : King of Sweden, he was killed on 6 November, 1632.

— p96 *Virgil, Lucan*: respectively Publius Vergilius Maro (70-19BC), writer of the *Aeneid, Georgics* and *Eclogues*, and effectively the national poet of Augustan Rome, and Marcus Annaeus Lucanus (39-65 AD), who fell out with Emperor Nero and was forced to commit suicide.

— *Tasso* : Torquato Tasso (1544-1595), born in Sorrento, was perhaps the most famous Italian poet of the 16th century, and author of the epic *Gerusalemme Liberata* (Jerusalem Freed, or Jerusalem Delivered), which had attracted the attention of English translators at an early stage.

— *Frankfurt* : Battle of Frankfurt (an der Oder) (1631) won by the Swedes.

— *Leipzig* : Battle of Leipzig (1642), otherwise known as Second Battle of Breitenfeld, this being some 5 miles NE of Leipzig. The Swedes defeated the Imperial army, which was commanded by the Austrian Archduke Leopold Wilhelm.

— *Würzburg* : taken by Gustavus Adolphus in 1631.

— *Tilly* : Johann Tserclaes, Count of Tilly (1559-1632): Imperial General, from what is now Belgium, in the Thirty Years' War; one of the two main commanders of the Imperial forces, with Wallenstein. Defeated by Gustanus Adolphus at Breitenfeld/Leipzig. Wonded at the Battle of Rain (am Lech), and died of tetanus 15 days later.

— *Lech* : Battle of Lech, also known as the Battle of Rain (1632), from the village of Rain on the River Lech, Bavaria.

— *Danube* : probably refers to the Battle of Landshut (a.k.a. Landeshut, 1634), where Protestant forces defeated an Imperial army. Landshut is in Bavaria, and is actually located on the banks of the Isar, a tributary of the Danube.

— *Rhine* : Prince Rupert of the Rhine (1619-1682), German soldier born in Prague, younger son of the Elector Palatine, Friedrich V, but also the nephew of King Charles I of England. Fought with the Protestant / Swedish forces in the Thirty Years' War, and later became Commander of the Royal Cavalry in the English Civil War, and finally the senior Royalist General, surrendering to Parliamentary forces after the fall of Bristol. In a colourful career he was later to serve with French forces, operate as a privateer in the Caribbean, and finally return to England and become a naval commander in the Anglo-Dutch wars. In his later years he was head of the Royal Navy.

— *Papenheim* : Gottfried Heinrich, Graf [Count] Pappenheim (1594-1632), a Bavarian general of the Imperial forces in the Thirty Years' War. He died on the same day, in the same battle as Gustavus Adolphus. See Lutzenfeld.

— *Wallenstein* : Bohemian general (1583-1634) in the service of the Holy Roman Empire during the Thirty Years' war. Also known as Valdstejna (Czech) and Waldstein (a German version of his Czech name). He was assassinated by one Walter Devereux, with the Emperor's approval – the latter having distrusted this able and ambitious military man.

— *Lutzenfeld* : the Battle of Lützen (1632), SW of Leipzig. Once again, a victory for the forces of the Protestant King Gustavus Adolphus, but the entire Protestant campaign was derailed by the death of the Swedish King, their greatest commander, on the battlefield. (Hence the poem's "posthume Victory".) This marked the end of Swedish supremacy in the battle against the Catholic imperial forces.

— *Austrian grasp*: the Emperor was Austrian.

— p97 *Shepherd's Paradise* : seems to imply that Townsend is the author of this masque, which has otherwise been assigned to the pen of Walter Montague. Carew knew both men.

— p98 *Carabins* : carbines, or rifles.

p99 Upon Master W. Montague
Walter "Wat" Montague (1604-1677) had a colourful life: he was employed as a spy by Buckingham, making a number of trips to France, and was captured there, and imprisoned. He returned to England in 1633, which may well be the date of the poem's composition. His masque, *Shepherd's Paradise* (but see above), was produced that same year. He went to Rome in 1639, and converted to Catholicism; became Chamberlain to the Queen, and was then thrown into the Tower. Banished in 1649, he relocated to Pontoise, where be became an Abbot.

— *smooth as when the halcyon builds her nest* : the *halcyon* was a mythical bird, said to have a nest floating at sea, from which it could charm the waves and the winds to calm.

— *Boreas* : in ancient Greek mythology, the god of the north wind, and god of winter. Usually depicted as a winged god.

— p100 *Æolus* : there are three different mythological characters of this name (or three variations of the one character), but the one that fits here is the one mentioned in the *Odyssey*, where he is known as the Keeper of the Winds. He gave Odysseus a bag full of captured winds to enable him to return to Ithaca.

— *Delphos* : from whom Delphi obtained its name. There are various legends, naming him as son of Poseidon, son of Apollo, etc.

p100 To Master W. Montague
Ostracism : a legal procedure in ancient Athens whereby a citizen could be expelled from the city for ten years.

p101 On the marriage of T.K. and C.C.
Thomas Killigrew and Cecilia Crofts, the latter of the Saxham Crofts, and a maid-of-honour to Queen Henrietta Maria, wife of King Charles I. The marriage took place in 1636, but Cecilia was to die in 1638, having borne one son, and is buried in Westminster Abbey.

p103 To a Lady
eyne : eyes.

p105 Upon my Lord Chief Justice…
Sir John Finch (1584-1660), who took up this post in 1634. A.W. is thought to be Anne Wentworth, third daughter of the Earl of Cleveland, and born in 1623. She married Lord Lovelace, Baron of Hurley, in 1638, when she was 15.

p108 To my friend G.N. from Wrest
Possibly Gilbert Neville. Wrest must be Wrest Park in Bedfordshire, home of the Grey family.

— p109 Favonius : a Roman wind god.
Vernal winds : Spring winds.

— *Of carved Marble, Touch, or Porphyry* : Basanites, a stone used for testing gold, was also known as "touch".

— p110 *Amalthea* : foster-mother of Zeus in Greek mythology.

— *Ceres* : Roman goddess of agriculture, grain and crops, fertility and motherhood.

— *Marble Tun* : marble barrel.

— *Bacchus* : Roman name of the Greek god, Dionysos. God of the grape harvest, wine, ritual madness, fertility, theatre and religious ecstasy.

p.111 *Vertumnus* : Roman god of seasons and change, as well as gardens and trees. He was a shape-shifter.

— *Pomona*: in Ovid's *Metamorphoses*, Pomona – goddess of fruitful abundance (her name derives from *pomum*, fruit) – was tricked into talking to Vertumnus, as the latter had appeared to her as an old woman. She had previously scorned the advances of two other woodland gods, but married Vertumnus after his stealthy advances.

— *Zephyr* : a light west wind.

— *Flora* : goddess of flowers and of the Spring.

— *Falerne* : Falernian wine was the most famous wine of ancient Rome, made of Aglianico grapes grown on the slopes of Mt. Falernus. The wine was from late-harvest grapes, and was then aged in amphorae for 15 years or more. The alcohol content must have been high, as Pliny the Elder recorded that it could be set alight. There were three varieties: dry, sweet and light.

p112 A New-year's gift to the King
Janus : god of beginnings and transitions; hence *January*.
Charles : the King.

— p113 *Bifront*: having two faces (like Janus).

p114 To the New Year for the Countess of Carlisle
See previous mention of the Countess in the note to p49.

p115 To My Honoured Friend Master Thomas May
This was prefaced to the printed version of *The Heir; a comedy as it was acted by the Company of revels*, 1620 (published 1622). Thomas May (1595-1650) translated Virgil and Lucan, and later adhered to the Parliamentary cause.

p116 To My Worthy Friend Master Geo. Sands
George Sandys (1578-1644) was seventh son of Edwin Sandys, Archbishop of York. He lived for some time in the Virginian colony and in Bermuda, and translated part of Ovid's *Metamorphoses* while in America. His *Paraphrase upon the Psalms* was published in 1636, with a new edition in 1638 that included Carew's commendatory verses.

p117 Golgotha : Calvary, place of Christ's crucifixion.

p118 To My Friend Henry, Lord Cary of Lepington
Eldest son of the Earl of Monmouth, whose title he inherited in 1639. His younger brother was Thomas Carey, who is **not** the author of this book. This poem was prefaced to *Romulus and Tarquin* (1637) a translation of Malvezzi's *Il Romulo* and *Il Tarquinio Superbo*.

— *Malvezzi* : Vergilio, Marchese (Marquis) de Malvezzi (1599-1654), briefly Ambassador to England.

— *Bembo* : Pietro Bembo (1470-1547), Cardinal, and also poet who wrote in Latin, and attempted to restore a pure classical style to writing in that language.

— *Varchi* : (1502-1562) Poet and historian.

— *Crusca* : the Academy of Florence which established the first dictionary of Italian.

p118 To My worthy friend, M. D'Avenant
William Davenant, or D'Avenant (1606-1668), poet and playwright whose godfather was said to have been William Shakespeare. He was made Poet Laureate in 1638, remained loyal to the royal cause and stayed in exile after the defeat of the royalists, but was captured while en route to America, and sentenced to death. Reputedly, he was saved by the intercession of John Milton.

— p119 *Beaumont* : Francis Beaumont (1584-1616), playwright best-known for *The Knight of the Burning Pestle* and for his many collaborations with John Fletcher.

—*Jonson* : Ben Jonson.

p120 To the Reader of Master William Davenant's Play
The play is *The Wits*, a comedy produced at Blackfriars Theatre in 1634, and then published in 1636, with these commendatory verses.

p121 To William Davenant, my Friend
This was prefaced to the first edition of Davenant's *Madagascar, with other Poems* (1638).
—*Dido*: Queen of Carthage in Virgil's *Aeneid*.
— *Homer's Ajax or Achilles*: Greek heroes in the *Iliad*.

— *Tale of Troy*: the *Iliad*.

— *Carthage Queen* : Dido, from the *Aeneid*.

p120 The Comparison
Leda's Swan: according to the Greek myth. Zeus appeared in the guise of a swan and seduced Leda, Queen of Sparta.

— *Jove*: Jupiter / Zeus, king of the gods.

p129-131 To the Painter
p130 *Pygmalion* – character from Ovid's *Metamorphoses*, a Cypriot sculptor who falls in love with a statue he had created.

p133 The Protestation
Lethe : one of the five rivers of Hades, the underworld, in Greek mythology. All who drank from its waters forgot everything. In Classical Greek the word actually means *oblivion* or *forgetfulness*.

p139 On Mistress N
Manuscript evidence suggests that Mistress N was one of the sisters Neville, Katherine and Mary, daughters of Sir Henry Neville.

— *green sickness* : known also in the 16th century as *chlorosis*, this is now termed Hypochromic anaemia, a condition in which the red blood cells are paler than normal. Like other kinds of anaemia, it can have its origins in an iron deficiency.

p139 Upon a mole...
Hyblas: Hybla was a town in ancient Sicily famed for its honey. More than one town went by this name.

p140 An Hymeneal Song
Wedding song for Lady Anne Wentworth, 3rd daughter of Thomas, Earl of Cleveland, and grand-daughter of Sir John Crofts of Saxham. Lord Lovelace: John, Lord Lovelace, Baron of Hurley. The marriage took place in 1638.

p147 To his mistress
canker'd. : Literally, infected as with canker, which is an ulceration of the lips or the mouth. It is also an open wound in a tree, or a disease of horses in which the hard part of the hoof becomes soft. It is thus a visible sign of illness.

p148 In praise of his Mistress
Po: a river in northern Italy.

p1479 To Celia
Ind: India / the Indies. The Indies are doubtless mentioned here as suggesting somewhere exotic and very distant, rather than being intended as a literal location.

Index of First Lines

Lightning Source UK Ltd.
Milton Keynes UK
UKOW02f1544210317

297145UK00001BA/26/P